W9-BXZ-303

Richard Rizzo

WENDY LESSER is the founder and editor of *The Threepenny Review,* which Adam Zagajewski has called "one of the most original literary magazines not only in the U.S. but also on the entire planet." She is the author of eight previous books of non-fiction and one novel. Her most recent book is the prizewinning *Music for Silenced Voices: Shostakovich and His Fifteen String Quartets.* She has written for *The New York Times Book Review,* the *London Review of Books, The Times Literary Supplement,* and other publications. She divides her time between Berkeley, California, and New York City.

ALSO BY WENDY LESSER

Music for Silenced Voices:
Shostakovich and His Fifteen Quartets

Room for Doubt

The Pagoda in the Garden (a novel)

Nothing Remains the Same: Rereading and Remembering

The Amateur: An Independent Life of Letters

A Director Calls

Pictures at an Execution

His Other Half: Men Looking at Women Through Art

The Life Below the Ground: A Study of the Subterranean
in Literature and History

Hiding in Plain Sight:
Essays in Criticism and Autobiography (editor)

The Genius of Language: Fifteen Writers Reflect
on Their Mother Tongues (editor)

Additional Praise for *Why I Read*

"We turn to a book like Lesser's not only to help us unravel the DNA of literature (what Hazlitt named the gusto in the soul of literature) but to commune with a mind abler than our own, to augment our own appreciation and understanding. . . . Wendy Lesser is a serious reader—a *quality* reader—and this book is a serious pleasure."

—William Giraldi, *The New York Times Book Review* (Editors' Choice)

"Reading Wendy Lesser is like attending a book club where the leader is an Olympic champion reader. Think the Dana Torres of page-turning . . . Just like your favorite book club, the discussion is brainy, it's personal, and it's occasionally off topic."

—*The Christian Science Monitor*

"In the tradition of E. M. Forster's *Aspects of the Novel* and James Wood's *How Fiction Works,* Lesser's *Why I Read* is an investigation of the mechanisms behind great literature. . . . Her tone is scholarly but conversational, and informed by her own obvious pleasure in reading."

—*The New Yorker*

"I began Wendy Lesser's *Why I Read: The Serious Pleasure of Books* with my usual yellow highlighter in hand, notepaper and pen at the ready, opening the reviewer's copy as I would for any normal assignment. By the time I'd finished, the notepaper was still mostly blank, but the thing in my hand resembled a brightly painted fan—every page saturated in color, with so many corners folded down the book had trouble staying closed. . . . [A] journey of pure pleasure."

—*San Francisco Chronicle*

WHY I READ

The Serious Pleasure of Books

WENDY LESSER

Picador

Farrar, Straus and Giroux

New York

www.picadorusa.com
www.twitter.com/picadorusa • www.facebook.com/picadorusa
picadorbookroom.tumblr.com

Picador® is a U.S. registered trademark and is used by Farrar, Straus and Giroux under license from Pan Books Limited.

For book club information, please visit www.facebook.com/picadorbookclub or e-mail marketing@picadorusa.com.

The Library of Congress has cataloged the Farrar, Straus and Giroux edition as follows:

Lesser, Wendy.
  Why I Read: The Serious Pleasure of Books / Wendy Lesser.
      pages   cm
  Includes index.
  ISBN 978-0-374-28920-1 (hardcover)
  ISBN 978-0-374-70981-5 (e-book)
  1. Books and reading.   2. Lesser, Wendy—Books and reading.   3. Literature—History and criticism.   I. Title.

Z1003 .L543 2014
028'.9—dc23

2013033000

Picador ISBN 978-1-250-06209-3

Picador books may be purchased for educational, business, or promotional use. For information on bulk purchases, please contact the Macmillan Corporate and Premium Sales Department at 1-800-221-7945, extension 5442, or write to specialmarkets@macmillan.com.

First published in the United States by Farrar, Straus and Giroux

First Picador Edition: January 2015

10 9 8 7 6 5 4 3 2 1

For Tim and Anne

It is art that *makes* life, makes interest, makes importance, for our consideration and application of these things, and I know of no substitute whatever for the force and beauty of its process. —Henry James, letter to H. G. Wells

So long as I remain alive and well I shall continue to feel strongly about prose style, to love the surface of the earth, and to take pleasure in solid objects and scraps of useless information. It is no use trying to suppress that side of myself. The job is to reconcile my ingrained likes and dislikes with the essentially public, non-individual activities that this age forces on all of us. —George Orwell, "Why I Write"

At least, thought Amalfitano, I've read thousands of books. At least I've become acquainted with the Poets and read the Novels. (The Poets, in Amalfitano's view, were those beings who flashed like lightning bolts, and the Novels were the stories that sprang from *Don Quixote*.) At least I've read. At least I can still read, he said to himself, at once dubious and hopeful. —Roberto Bolaño, *Woes of the True Policeman*

CONTENTS

WHY I READ

PROLOGUE: WHY I READ

It's not a question I can completely answer. There are abundant reasons, some of them worse than others and many of them mutually contradictory. To pass the time. To savor the existence of time. To escape from myself into someone else's world. To find myself in someone else's words. To exercise my critical capacities. To flee from the need for rational explanations.

And even the obvious reasons may not be the real ones. My motives remain obscure to me because reading is, to a certain extent, a compulsion. As with all compulsions, its sources prefer to stay hidden.

In any case, when I ask myself why I read literature, I am not really asking about motivation. I am asking what I get from it: what delights I have received over the years, what rewards I can expect to glean. This I am sure of. The rewards are enormous. But they too tend toward the intangible, and sometimes the inexpressible. I have tried to express some of them here, but without any hope of being all-encompassing. Partial coverage—a flashlight shining into a dark room, briefly illuminating what sits on the rows of shelves—is all I can realistically aim for.

When it comes to literature, we are all groping in the
dark, even the writer. Especially the writer. And that is a
good thing—maybe one of the best things about literature.
It's always an adventure of some kind. Even the second or
third or tenth time you read it, a book can surprise you, and
to discover a new writer you love is like discovering a whole
new country. Some countries, like the novels of Nathanael
West or J. G. Farrell or E. M. Forster, are only the size of a
small island, because their author died young or dried up early.
Others, like the novels of Anthony Trollope or Émile Zola,
seem to cover a whole continent, requiring years just to map
out and superficially explore. One kind of land mass is not
better than another (though they do tend to appeal to different tastes), and whichever you prefer, there are always more
out there. You will never reach the end.

I suppose if I had to give a one-word answer to the question of why I read, that word would be pleasure. The kind of
pleasure you can get from reading is like no other in the
world. People even get pleasure out of reading bad books,
and I deplore this, but that is only because those books are
not to my taste. You will deplore some of the works I hold up
as models in this book, and that is not only sensible, but inevitable. Because reading is such an individual act, the pleasures we derive from literature—even which books we are
willing to call "literature"—will not be identical. That is as it
should be. Reading can result in boredom or transcendence,
rage or enthusiasm, depression or hilarity, empathy or contempt, depending on who you are and what the book is and
how your life is shaping up at the moment you encounter it.
This effect will be particular to each person, and it will
change over time, just as the person changes over time—and
the richer and more complicated the book is, the more this
will be true.

I have tried, in this book, to cast a wide net in my definition of literature, looking at plays, poems, and essays as well as novels and stories. Along with more traditional literary forms, I have included mysteries and science fiction, memoirs and journalism, the only requirement being that the book be well-written enough to last through multiple readings, not to mention multiple generations of readers. With my contemporaries, of course, I have had to guess at this: I possess no magical powers that enable me to see the literary future.

I do, however, have a time-travel machine of sorts, in the form of the literature of the past. Just about everything I know about nineteenth-century England comes out of novels. Ditto for nineteenth-century Russia, late-nineteenth-century France, and twentieth-century India. Those fictional images and experiences are now so much a part of my own mind that superimposed reality pales by comparison. Jane Austen's Bath is more present to me than the tourist-laden city I have actually visited, and Gogol's Nevsky Prospect is more memorable than the mundane boulevard I saw when I finally got to St. Petersburg. I will never experience Bombay from the viewpoint of its slums, as Rohinton Mistry allows me to do; I will never feel at home in the actual Paris the way I do in the Paris of Balzac, Zola, or Proust. And even certain parts of America—William Faulkner's South, Willa Cather's Southwest, Ross Macdonald's Southern California—are more familiar to me in their literary form than they are as geographical entities I have or might set foot in.

Does this mean I am in retreat from reality? I don't think so—or not, anyway, more than the average person who sits at a computer screen, or watches television, or consumes daily newspapers and weekly magazines. We all live much of our lives at one remove. Perhaps this has always been true, but at the present moment it seems more true than ever. One is tempted to blame technology for this: the internet, social media, email. But there is no doing without these things, now that they have arrived, and there is no point in just being resistant. We must live in this world.

I live in it with, and through, literature. That, I suppose, is what I am hoping to transmit—that sense of connection with something other than oneself and one's friends and one's life in this time. Reading literature is a way of reaching back to something bigger and older and different. It can give you the feeling that you belong to the past as well as the present, and it can help you realize that your present will someday be someone else's past. This may be disheartening, but it can also be strangely consoling at times.

And if the sense of connection we get through literature is an illusory one, how is that any different from most of the kinds of connection we feel these days? Reading has, at any rate, the virtue of being one-to-one. It's just you and the book, enclosed within a private space; in some ways that means it's just you, alone with an inert object that you are temporarily bringing to life. So within and beside that palpable sense of connection, that awareness of a vast community of readers and writers stretching backward and forward through time, lies something that seems paradoxically at odds with it: that is, a firm, resilient feeling of detachment. Nothing takes you out of yourself the way a good book does, but at the same time nothing makes you more aware of yourself as a solitary creature, possessing your own particular tastes, memories, associations, beliefs. Even as it fully engages you with another mind (or maybe many other minds, if you count the characters' as well as the author's), reading remains a highly individual act. No one will ever do it precisely the way you do.

.

I hope that, in the course of reading this small book about a rather large subject, you will come to think of it as a conversation we are having. A conversation does not need to have two people speaking to each other in the same room. Nor does it need to have RSS feeds, rapidly tweeted responses, or any of the other contemporary manifestations of interactivity. Some of my most memorable conversations have occurred in mute communion with absent authors. Silence can be a form of response, and it can also be conducive to response: I find that the enduring stillness of a printed page often sets my thoughts racing in a way that more active forms of communication may not. True, the absent writers of such pages cannot hear my reactions to their work, but that doesn't bother either of us. They so often seem to have anticipated my thoughts that I feel welcomed into the conversation even when I am saying nothing.

And so it will turn out, I hope, between you and me. You too are bringing something to this conversation—your attention, your memories, your interpretations of what I am saying, your reflections on the books you have read. You are my silent partner in this enterprise. As I make observations and assertions, you give your assent or withhold it, according to your own opinions. Sometimes I may persuade you, and sometimes you may resist. In either case, the conversation continues for as long as you are reading the book, and possibly after.

I have never consciously thought about audience before, with any of my previous books. If asked, I would have said something like "I just write for myself and presume that there are others like me," or "That is the marketing department's concern." But with this book—perhaps because it so often contemplates that very relationship between writer and reader, speaker and spoken to, in the works of literature I have loved—I find myself wondering who you are. Are you a young person just starting out on a lifetime of reading, or are you an older reader who has already acquired fixed tastes and preferences? Do you come from a background similar to mine, or are we completely unlike in all sorts of ways? I would hope that the answer might be "all of the above," and perhaps it can be, for the written word, at least as embodied in the English language, allows "you" to be both singular and plural. It is not only the writer who can say, with Walt Whitman, "I am large, I contain multitudes." That truth applies to readers as well.

A word here about the idea of truth. I will invoke the notion often, and yet I will not be able to define it for you, except by example. It is one of my touchstones for judging literature, this question of whether a writer is telling me the truth or not. (We will not, for the moment, go into what truth is, because this is something that can vary from author to author. The question of whether truth is in fact single or multiple, capitalized or lowercase, is part of what each good writer is trying to answer truthfully.) You will find the word circling back at you throughout this book, especially in the chapter about authority, but also when I talk about character, about innovative forms, about the relation of the reader's "you" to the writer's "I," about the nature of translation, about grand or intimate perspectives. Whenever the idea surfaces, it is meant to apply equally well to fiction and to nonfiction. Reality and truth, history and truth, are in this respect separable. My use of the term is not arbitrary, but it is elusive, and I hope you will bear with me and allow the process of truth-defining to be cumulative rather than absolute. As far as I know, that is the only way things can work in literature.

I have said that I aimed to make this book conversational, and I do. Clarity is a great virtue. But sometimes things cannot be made instantly clear, and there are times when a form of heightened concentration may be required. This is one of the favors literature has done for me—it has taught me the pleasures of close attention. A work of commentary or criticism is not necessarily a work of literature, but it can aspire to that condition and be the better for it. I aspire, in this little book, toward the qualities I have admired in novels and poetry, including the compression, the indirection, the inherent connections, the organic shape.

There are no topics that absolutely had to be covered in this book. There are no essential facts that I needed to convey to you about literature. There are certain questions that I have long been curious about, and that I wanted to answer for myself as well as for you—questions about the nature of suspense, for instance, and why we feel it even when we know what will happen; questions about our connection to specific characters, as well as their connection to their author; questions about the kinds of sentences that bring a novel into being, or usher us out of it; questions about belief, and doubt, and the historically true, and the fictionally imagined. And then there are the works of literature that have raised these questions in my mind, and through which I hope to answer them. Whether they are fourteen-line poems or six-hundred-page novels, all of these literary works contain multitudes. They refuse to fit neatly into separate chapters and instead reappear as needed, offering their answers to each different question in turn. Nor do they present themselves on demand: they are willful creatures whose movements I do not completely control. Thus I may admire Tolstoy as much as I admire Dostoyevsky (even more, perhaps, if I have just finished reading *War and Peace*), and yet it is Dostoyevsky who insists on returning again and again to this book, whether I am talking about intimacy or authority or plot, while Tolstoy remains largely behind the scenes, holding himself aloof. "I can call spirits from the vasty deep," boasts a character in Shakespeare's *Henry IV, Part One*, to which another character sensibly answers, "Why, so can I, or so can any man; / But will they come when you do call for them?"

So the book has taken its shape organically, as the various willfulnesses, mine and those of the literary sources, battle with each other and resistantly work together. Yet out of this conflict has come some kind of order. I like to picture the final shape of the book as something like a spiral, on which you and I are progressing upward (or perhaps downward) but also round and round. Each new chapter represents a new level of the spiral, so we know we are getting somewhere; and yet we are always circling around the same elongated core, greeting now-familiar works as we pass by them once again. There is movement, but it is not exactly forward movement. There is repetition, but each time the repeated material is seen from a different view. And there is simultaneously a feeling of internal division and a sense of natural flow, since each chamber of the spiral remains connected to the one that came before it and the one that will come after. Happenstance rather than certainty governs the process of growth. Yet once it is finished, the structure will seem to have arrived at its only possible shape, so that there will be some sense of completion, I hope, even in its open-endedness.

ONE

CHARACTER AND PLOT

I had meant to keep these two things separate. I intended to start with a chapter about character and then move on, in the next chapter, to plot, since that is pretty much the order in which I choose what I want to read. The two labels had a kind of inevitability in my mind, as if mathematicians had discovered them in nature. And it's true that writers and readers and teachers and critics have been using these terms for such a long time now that it would be hard to do without them. Yet they turn out not to be oppositional categories, or even fully separable ones. As I discovered when I began to press harder on the distinction, it doesn't make sense to think in terms of plot *versus* character: plot modifies character and character modifies plot, and there can be no meaningful version of one that exists purely without the other.

Henry James (who always gets there before me) observed in his sharp, generous essay about the novels of Anthony Trollope:

> If he had taken sides on the droll, bemuddled opposition between novels of character and novels of plot, I can imagine him to have said (except that he never expressed himself

in epigrams), that he preferred the former class, inasmuch as
character in itself is plot, while plot is by no means character. It is more safe indeed to believe that his great good
sense would have prevented him from taking an idle con-
troversy seriously. Character, in any sense in which we can
get at it, is action, and action is plot, and any plot which
hangs together, even if it pretend to interest us only in the
fashion of a Chinese puzzle, plays upon our emotion, our
suspense, by means of personal references. We care what
happens to people only in proportion as we know what
people are.

And, he might have added, we know what people are only by
seeing what they do when confronted with what happens to
them: this is what James means when he says that character,
"in any sense in which we can get at it," is action, or plot.

One has only to look at his own novels to see how this
works. Characters like Isabel Archer, Kate Croy, and Maggie
Verver, though they may spend whole chapters musing to
themselves, essentially think in the same way they speak: ra-
tionally, socially, effortfully. Despite James's reputation as a
novelist of great psychological depth, there are virtually no
scenes in which he peers beneath the verbal surface, telling us
that whereas So-and-so *appeared* to think this, she *really* thought
that. Behavior is the manifestation of thought, in James. In the
few cases where his characters attempt to think deviously—as
does, for instance, Mrs. Gereth in *The Spoils of Poynton*—they
are almost always mistaken, or misguided, or at the very least
misled as to the efficacy of their own wishes and beliefs. In
this respect, the purely psychological interior is not the place
where James's deepest truths dwell. Nor do his characters
dream, for the most part. If they have an unconscious, it is as
invisible to them as it is to us.

It is not just a matter of *our* knowing these people through their actions. That is how they come to know themselves. Isabel Archer does not fully define herself to herself—does not, in that sense, arrive at her long-sought fate—until, at the end of *The Portrait of a Lady*, she renounces her own hard-won freedom and returns to Rome for the sake of her step-daughter, Pansy. Kate Croy, in *The Wings of the Dove*, does not realize how deeply she hates the squalor of poverty until she finds herself manipulating her fiancé into marriage with a dying heiress. And Maggie Verver, in *The Golden Bowl*, has no sense of the reserves of her own psychological fortitude, no awareness of how much power she is capable of exerting, until she sets out to separate her husband from his mistress, who happens to be her beloved father's wife. These women do not come ready-packaged with a character that accompanies them through life, like a kit-bag of charms carried by the generic hero of a fairy tale. On the contrary, they become their characters—they develop into them—by facing up to the various things that life throws at them, some as a result of chance and others stemming directly from their own actions. But even to distinguish chance from self-imposed destiny is to belie the atmosphere of a James novel, where character is both forged and manifested through its confrontation with all kinds of events—events which, as this perspicacious author repeatedly suggests, arise from an indistinguishable melding of self, environment, history, will, and coincidence.

Henry James's chosen task, as a novelist, was to locate such moments of self-creation, self-definition, self-discovery—call it what you will—in the often superficial, frequently decep-tive, socially complex life of his times. It is not always a pretty sight, this moment at which the person finds out who or what she is, but it is always interesting, which is why the last hun-dred pages of a James novel invariably zoom by in a flood of suspense. If this payoff for the character, and for us, comes at the end, for the novelist himself it always began much earlier, at the dinner party or the polite gathering where, in the casual conversations taking place around him, he first caught a glimpse of his precious *donnée*, that "given" item of news or hearsay from which he could begin to weave his fictional web. To see him at home after the party as he writes up his almost-nightly notebook entries, working out the details of what he has captured on the fly, is practically to feel in one's own body the palpable thrill of authorial discovery. The initial stimulus is never sufficient, the shred of gossip never enough: he has to work it over and over, teasing and tinkering and toying with it, until what he was handed becomes what he wants. The given turns into the wrought-upon, as the self imposes its own nature on the bare events it is faced with. It is a recapitulation of the very process his characters go through.

It was at a dinner on December 23, 1893, that James first heard, from a Mrs. Anstruther-Thompson, the core of the tale that ultimately became *The Spoils of Poynton*—a "small and ugly matter" involving a young laird who, upon his marriage, planned to dispossess his widowed mother of her house and all its beautiful possessions, as he had a legal right to do. The plot, as we now have it in the novel, is practically all there from the beginning: the mother's hatred of the new wife, her removal of the precious objects, the threat of litigation, and so on. But the elusive heart of the story is still evading James as late as the fall of 1895, nearly two years later. On October 15, he uses his notebook entry to explore the problem. "What does she do then?—how does she work, how does she achieve her heroism?" he asks himself about the character of Fleda Vetch (a creation of his own, distinctly *not* a figure in the initial dinner-table story). "It's the question of *how* she takes care of it that is the tight knot of my *donnée*," he goes on. And then, before our very eyes, he loosens that knot by worrying at it:

> That confronts me with the question of the action Fleda exercises on Mrs. Gereth and of how she exercises it. My old idea was that she worked, as it were, on her feelings. Well, eureka! I think I have found it—I think I see the little interesting turn and the little practicable form . . . How a little click of perception, of this sort, brings back to me all the strange sacred time of my thinkings-out, this way, pen in hand, of the stuff of my little theatrical trials . . . My new little notion was to represent Fleda as committing—for drama's sake—some broad effective stroke of her own. But that now looks to me like a mistake: I've got hold, very possibly, of the tail of the right thing. Isn't the right thing to make Fleda simply work upon Mrs. Gereth, but work in an interesting way?

And here, with his metaphor of the "tail," he suggests how he is being led by something outside himself, is merely following an idea that has been thrust upon him with that nearly audible "click of perception." Is this process internal or external, character-driven or plot-driven? The question makes no sense, because the two are inseparable.

Still, I would have to say that for me character is always at the forefront. I cannot enjoy even a plain old mystery if the people (the detectives *and* the killers, but especially the detectives) do not on some level strike me as persuasive. And in this view I am supported, it turns out, by that grandmaster of plotting, Wilkie Collins. "It may be possible, in novel-writing," he wrote in the 1861 preface to his wildly popular thriller *The Woman in White*, "to present characters successfully without telling a story; but it is not possible to tell a story successfully without presenting characters: their existence, as recognisable realities, being the sole condition on which the story can effectively be told. The only narrative which can hope to lay a strong hold on the attention of readers, is a narrative which interests them about men and women—for the perfectly obvious reason that they are men and women themselves."

To be persuasive, a character need not necessarily adhere to the rules of humdrum reality. Nor need she be a fully shaped human figure with descriptive qualities attached. Sometimes, as in a poem, she can simply be a voice. But what she *does* need to have, if she is to persuade us of her reality, is a plausible relationship to her own context. That context resides in the content of the work of literature (its situation, its setting, its plot), but also in its form, by which I mean its language, its diction, its mode of address. So there are at least two kinds of surrounding environment: the one the character perceives, because she exists there as a real person, and another of which she generally remains oblivious, because it defines her as a fictional character. Both collaborate to shape her personality and our response to it.

Every character springs from and belongs to his own specific world, and though he may be successfully relocated from that context (as Hamlet, for instance, is relocated to an existential-absurdist performance in Tom Stoppard's *Rosencrantz and Guildenstern Are Dead*), he will not be the same character in the new setting, even if he is still given his old lines. Because the tendrils that hold him to his original work are at once so delicate and so firmly wound, it doesn't really make sense to distinguish a character from the other literary elements—situation, language, event, other characters—that surround and create him. Yet writers and readers have always made precisely this distinction. Perhaps we insist on it because we ourselves, *as* selves, feel separate from and independent of all the multitudinous factors that have gone into our own making and continue to influence our actions. To the extent that we believe ourselves to be autonomous individuals in the world, we tend, or at least wish, to grant the same autonomy to literary characters.

Some characters certainly seem more autonomous than others. Memorability, that repeated capacity to leap out of the general mist of our past reading and take center stage in our minds, is often but not always the sign of a great literary character. The characters that stick with us for weeks and months and even years after we close the book tend to be larger or at least more exaggerated than life, but they are also lifelike: they come back to us, in part, because we are reminded of them by the people we meet as we go through the rest of our lives. It's not so much that we encounter these characters in the flesh as that we encounter their memorable qualities transferred onto living people, sometimes including ourselves.

This is especially true of Dickens's characters, and it is the minor characters in Dickens, the ones that re-enact their distinctive habits over and over again, who tend to be most memorable in this way. The figure I recall most often from *David Copperfield* (and it is a novel filled with ghoulishly memorable characters: Mr. Micawber, Mr. Murdstone, Steerforth) is the eminently creepy Uriah Heep, who oozes oily fake-helpfulness and disgusting false humility even as he ushers his kind, oblivious employer into the poorhouse. If the other characters come back to me once a year or so, Uriah Heep recurs ten times as often. Nobody in life is *exactly* like Uriah Heep, of course, but there are many who share at least some of his irritating qualities. And such is Dickens's power that when I meet these Heepish people, I can somehow imagine them rubbing their clammy hands together and calling themselves "'umble" even if that is something they would never do.

We recognize Uriah Heep by the way he expresses himself, but even characters without language can be memorably embodied in words. In literature as in life, the nonverbal or the preverbal can be powerful and moving figures with their own particular points of view. Anyone who has ever owned a dog, and many who have not, will consider the dog Bendicò a central character in Giuseppe Tomasi di Lampedusa's marvelous novel *The Leopard*. His master, the Prince, certainly does; and so, it seems, did his author. In a postscript to a letter Lampedusa wrote about his only novel, belatedly added to the outside of the envelope, he scribbled, "N.B.: the dog Bendicò is a vitally important character and practically the key to the novel." Even without this scribbled note, we would sense this, for it is the stuffed carcass of the long-dead dog, tossed away onto the dustheap, that ends this sad, funny, feelingly ironic novel about the decline of the Sicilian aristocracy.

The ten-month-old baby whose point of view is briefly taken by the narrator of *The Old Wives' Tale* is another case in point. Though he is a much more temporary figure than Bendicò (in that he is only a wordless baby for a relatively short time: like most of us, he soon grows out of it), he is quite notable during the brief moment when Arnold Bennett captures him, lying on a soft woolen shawl laid over his parents' hearthrug. "For ten months," Bennett tells us, "he had never spent a day without making experiments on this shifting universe in which he alone remained firm and stationary. The experiments were chiefly conducted out of idle amusement, but he was serious on the subject of food. Lately the behavior of the universe in regard to his food had somewhat perplexed him, had indeed annoyed him."

In other words, he is being weaned. Only a single page of this long novel is devoted to the baby's viewpoint, but in it we see the hearth fire, the family dog, and the surrounding giant adults from his exhilarating, strangely philosophical, endlessly wondering perspective, before Bennett returns us to the mundane life of his parents. This single page is the one that has most strongly stayed with me through all my many decades of reading and rereading this book. Yet it was only on my last reading that I realized this baby eventually grows up to be the character who could be Arnold Bennett's own jaundiced self-portrait—a skeptical, cosmopolitan young man who fails to be sufficiently interested in the lives of the two women who are at the heart of the book, his mother and his aunt. But even if this is indeed an autobiographical character (and of that we can never be sure), Bennett did not use the faculty of memory to create that baby on the hearthrug. One can't, after all, remember one's own ten-month-old existence in detail, and this version of the experience is largely projection and imagination. That is as it should be, for the passage *feels* interior even as it proclaims with its language that it is not.

Lampedusa's Bendicò and Bennett's baby (to which one could add the anthropomorphic tumbleweed in Andrei Platonov's astonishing story "Soul") are novelties: great novelties, irreplaceable novelties, but not what we normally think of when we think of literary characters. They show what certain authors can do even with seemingly unpromising character material; they chasten us in regard to our usual presumptions about psychological complexity. And they make us realize, once again, how closely a fictional character is tied to whatever surrounds him—how much is needed, in the way of scenery, action, and interaction with others, to bring even a single tiny character to life.

•

Or to kill him off. When Henry James refers to plots that "pretend to interest us only in the fashion of a Chinese puzzle," he is alluding, I take it, to mystery and thriller plots. In his own time, that would have meant the mysteries of Wilkie Collins and, somewhat later, Arthur Conan Doyle; by the early twentieth century, he might have had access to John Buchan's brilliant thrillers, which began to appear just before James died. But it was not until the middle of the twentieth century that we received a flood of masterpieces in this vein, culminating in works such as those of Eric Ambler and Patricia Highsmith (to give just two examples—and very different examples at that, since one writer belongs firmly to the espionage-thriller camp, while the other specializes in the domestic murder mystery). Sentence by sentence, a novel like *A Coffin for Dimitrios* or *Ripley Under Ground* is as good as almost any book written during that time, and I venture to say we will be reading these novels for as long as people read John Updike or Toni Morrison.

In fact, there are certain things that thrillers can do better than serious novels. What these are will depend partly on the country of origin and the historical period, but in the late twentieth and early twenty-first centuries, in America and Western Europe, one of those things is definitely politics. When the serious novel of today attempts to cover subjects like terrorism, global warming, international financial shenanigans, civil unrest, and government corruption, the political side of the novel tends to feel like a superimposition pasted onto the "real" theme of a psychologically realistic interior life. In such novels, the parts about the characters' love affairs or family conflicts or tense work environments ring absolutely true, because that is what contemporary authors of naturalistic fiction have trained themselves to think about. But when they extend themselves into the larger political arena, the novels tend to go off the rails: the violent deaths and conspiratorial plots feel slightly cartoonish, especially when set beside the slowly accumulating, carefully investigated psychological portraits of the main characters.

In contrast, the novel that sets out to be a pure thriller takes as its starting point the violence or corruption of the political world. Such a novel has characters—in Ambler's case, for instance, they can be quite amusing and sympathetic characters, in an ironic, low-key way—but these characters do not exist primarily to display to us their personal, private, domestic inner lives. Instead, they function as players in the international scene: sometimes by mistake, to be sure, when an erroneous identification or a misunderstood message catches them up in the intrigue, but more often because they have worked in some capacity that connects them to the political world, as journalist or spy or government official of some kind. And this experience means that when violent deaths and mortal threats impinge on their lives, the events mesh naturally with their personalities. It is not just that they are equipped to deal with such things, but that they are practically *expecting* to deal with them, which means that we in turn, as readers, have this expectation as well. Instead of feeling tacked on in a well-intentioned but finally unsuccessful way, the political aspects of thriller novels feel integral to the plots. And if they are "good enough" thrillers—that is, works that satisfy a fairly high standard of literary style, as many do, despite or perhaps even because of their plainspokenness—we can read them with a kind of interest that is comparable to, though very different from, the interest we might bring to more purely psychological novels.

All novels are premised on a certain degree of suspense:

we keep reading because we want to find out how things turn out. In mystery novels, it's just that the contract with the reader is slightly more explicit. By the end of the book, we are assured, we will not only know everything of importance, but we will also be able to renounce any future concern about the fates of the characters involved. According to this contract, there will be no plotlines left dangling—as there so notably are, for instance, in the last sentence of Henry James's *The Bostonians*, where he says of his heroine's emotional tears: "It is to be feared that with the union, so far from brilliant, into which she was about to enter, these are not the last she was destined to shed." The marriage for which we have on some level been hoping throughout the novel, though in a somewhat mixed and perhaps skeptical way, has arrived to seal the plot of *The Bostonians*, but it turns out that this is only the beginning of another plot, one that we won't be around to witness. James's novels often end this way. A decision has been reached, an option has been closed off; the plot is, in that sense, terminated. But since life always offers more decisions, more options, we know that something else is going to happen to these characters after we leave them, and what that will be, we cannot really guess. Even when the authorial voice seems willing to prophesy, we can't fully trust it. After all, from whose point of view is Verena Tarrant's marriage to the ambitious, impoverished, irrepressible Basil Ransom considered "so far from brilliant"? Whose anxieties are expressed in the politely reticent "it is to be feared"—Verena's, about her own potential happiness, or society's, about her choice of husband? How strongly can we take the word "destined" when it comes to us couched in such ironic, particular, socially placed and therefore nonauthoritative language? In this final sentence, is James speaking to us in his own person, or as the ventriloquist of the society he's somewhat mockingly representing?

There are no firm answers to questions like these, and to answer "Both" is simply to beg them.

The mystery novel, as a rule, ends more firmly than this. It asks a straightforward question—which might be "Who committed the crime?" or possibly "Will the murderer be caught and punished, or will he escape?"—and then it proceeds to answer that question to our complete satisfaction. There are notable exceptions to this pattern, such as Per Wahlöö and Maj Sjöwall's *Rosanna*, where we never discover who committed the murder, or Jo Nesbø's *Redbreast*, which solves one aspect of its mystery plot but leaves an equally important element unresolved. But even these exceptions confirm the rule, by hastening on to multiple sequels in which the plots *do* get tied up, as if to say to us, "Yes, yes, you've been very good, tolerating this amount of ambiguity, but we promise not to ask it of you again."

The mystery, despite its general gruesomeness, is designed to reassure. It asserts the existence of an author who knows the answers (who has almost certainly, in fact, arrived at those answers before constructing the plot) and who will eventually give them to us. Of course, there are exceptions to this rule, too. John le Carré's Smiley books reassure us with their control—of plot, of language, of "tradecraft"—even as they undermine any faith we might have in the governmental powers-that-be, for in George Smiley's world the worst offenses always turn out to come from inside his own security-keeping system. And in Patricia Highsmith's Ripley novels, the standard version of reassurance gets turned on its head: here the murderer himself is the continuing character, and the investigating officers are just flies to be brushed off as each new episode passes. Playing on our own indwelling anxieties, taunting us with the nerve-wracking possibility that Ripley might be apprehended, Highsmith pushes our strange desire to empathize with a villain about as far as it can go, and that turns out to be very far indeed. We feel, reading her books, as if something bad we have done will be exposed and our guilt will be revealed. (She may *seem* to be talking about Ripley, but from our point of view she is really talking about us.) But even here, a kind of reassurance arrives at the end, because Ripley always vanquishes the police investigation and survives to kill again, just as Smiley solves the crime even when he can't bring the true criminals, his MI6 superiors, to justice. Is this reassurance, or its opposite? In the best mysteries, there is always a residue— of doubt, of anxiety, of concern about our social welfare. It is this residue which distinguishes the rereadable mysteries from the run-of-the-mill one-timers.

Perhaps it will seem perverse of me, in a book devoted to the subject of literature, to refer repeatedly to murder mysteries, a notoriously trashy form. But quality is not hierarchical. Judgments can always be made at any level; and though there are certainly good books and bad books in the world, they do not line up neatly according to rank, with good books filling the approved high genres and bad books the despised lower ones. If only stick figures inhabited the novels of Wilkie Collins and Patricia Highsmith (not to mention John Buchan, Ross Macdonald, Per Wahlöö and Maj Sjöwall, Henning Mankell, and all the other great mystery writers of the last couple of centuries), our interest in those books would greatly diminish. They would become simply like crossword puzzles, something ingeniously designed to kill time. Instead, they constitute one of the more essential forms of reading. Our own literary tradition might be said to have begun with the investigation of a murder (I'm thinking of Sophocles' *Oedipus Rex*: yet another story, like Jim Thompson's *The Killer Inside Me*, where the detective turns out to be the murderer), and I suspect it will end that way, if it ever does.

Dostoyevsky did his best to push it all toward an ending—both literature *and* the murder mystery—in his final novel, *The Brothers Karamazov*. There is a murder here which provides the engine of the plot, but does anyone recall the solution? No, because the solution is not what's important. If I ask you to remember several years after reading the novel whether Dmitri Karamazov killed his father, you might not be able to tell me the correct answer. That is, you will possibly think, as I did at the beginning of my recent rereading, that Dmitri committed the crime. The novel itself does not come down firmly on this question. It suggests that someone else was the guilty party, but it also implies that Dmitri *could* have done it, was morally capable of it, and therefore felt and acted guilty for a reason. (But then, Dmitri exists to experience guilt: that capacity, that outright need, is the essential element in his character.) We may continue reading the novel partly to find out who killed the horribly embarrassing, graspingly avaricious, ludicrously lustful old Karamazov—a singularly repellent and not-at-all-missed character to whom Dostoyevsky has wryly given his own first name, Fyodor—but if this is the only reason we are reading it, we will find *The Brothers Karamazov* a bizarrely unsatisfying work of fiction, filled with inexplicable digressions and seemingly endless speeches. We care about the novel because of what it tells us about Alyosha, Ivan, and Dmitri, those three brothers who are simultaneously themselves and larger than themselves.

Dostoyevsky tests to the limit the idea that evil characters are the most memorable, because in Dostoyevsky (as in Shakespeare, but even more so) the violent, destructive, self-loathing characters are the ones we are most drawn to. This is obviously true of *Crime and Punishment*, where the murderer

Raskolnikov is the central character, the focus of our deepest sympathetic interest. But it is also true of a strange work like *Demons*, which seems at first not even to be a novel at all, but rather a series of pointless conversations—about radical politics, domestic alliances, intellectual disappointments, petty rivalries, and everything else that made up nineteenth-century provincial Russian life. Yet even here the villainous characters stand out: not just the petty demons who enact all the devious crimes, though they are interesting in their own right, but above all the large-souled villain, the fascinating Stavrogin, who cannot help punishing himself for, but also with, his cruelty to women.

Stavrogin is the kind of character who can only exist in a Dostoyevsky novel. However much his characteristics may have been borrowed from real people (and Joseph Frank, in his masterful biography of Dostoyevsky, goes into great detail about who those models might have been), he stands apart as an unduplicated, unduplicatable figure, unlike anyone we will ever encounter in the flesh. With his intense self-hatred nestling beside his loathing for the rest of society, his profound sense of honor coexisting with his tendency to lie and deceive, and his moral corruption underlying and perhaps even reinforcing his supreme attractiveness, Stavrogin is a captivating original. Intelligence is not enough to explain his appeal (though it helps: a stupid Stavrogin would be inconceivable). Nor is physical beauty, because *we* can't actually see him, though the women who flock to him in the novel may in part be responding to that. In contrast to the distinctly life-sized figures who surround him in his mother's village—that anxious and commanding mother herself, her saintly young servant-companion, Stavrogin's ridiculous and impoverished old tutor, the tutor's scoundrel of a son, the marriageable daughter of neighboring landowners, the local radicals and spies, the pretentious village bureaucrats, even the idiot-girl to whom Stavrogin turns out to be married—he seems to glow with an excess of reality. They are all believable, and often pitiable, and in some cases loathsome, but he is something more than that: utterly present to us, yet beyond the reach of our normal, cathartic, fictionally inspired feelings. It is as if we can do nothing for him, because his fate is completely predetermined by his own personality, his own situation, and so we are helpless in the face of him. (Of course, it is literally true that we can do nothing for *any* fictional character, but our feelings tell us otherwise; in Stavrogin's case, they tell us the truth.)

On the whole, literature—in this respect much like history, or for that matter daily life—draws us toward the kinds of people who dominate, or at least attempt to dominate, their own circumstances. I'm thinking now not only of Stavrogin, but also of other great characters like Henry James's Kate Croy, or Hilary Mantel's Thomas Cromwell, or Jane Austen's Elizabeth Bennet, or Shakespeare's Cleopatra, or Tolstoy's Prince Andrei. These memorable figures all forcefully, or at any rate willfully, take certain actions that result in their having the lives they ultimately have. (And this is true even of the great characters who reign by their inactivity: think of Melville's Bartleby, for instance, or Goncharov's Oblomov, both of whom issue a comprehensive "No" to the routines of other people's existence.) One might say of these people that they make their own plots. And the suspense, for us, lies in seeing how they will negotiate all the different fixities that confront them: not only the author's willful predeterminations, and not just history's oblivious ones, but also the relentless immovability of their own characters.

·

One source of suspense is not knowing how things turn out, but an equally powerful source is knowing how they turn out and waiting for that to happen. There are certain novels that hinge, in part, on this kind of foreknowledge: their authors actually let us know the plot beforehand, not so much to ruin suspense as to heighten it. In Richard Ford's *Canada*, for instance, the elderly narrator, reflecting back on his childhood, tells us in the novel's first sentence that his parents robbed a bank, and then tells us again, repeatedly over the course of many pages, until we finally get to the event itself, about halfway through the book. At that point, having had something definite to look forward to, we find ourselves in freefall, with no certainty at all about what will happen next. Plot takes over, but not wholly: the role of memory is still ever-present, and we are never allowed to forget that the endangered young boy in the story turned into the older man who is telling us the tale. The novel as a whole possesses a cunning and unusual combination of forward movement and retrospective musing, with the result that the anxiety of the suspense somehow becomes infused with, or confused with, the calm of remembering.

In a different way, Shirley Hazzard's omniscient narrator in *The Transit of Venus* gives us forecasts we don't know how to use until the very end of the novel. Quite early in the plot, this voice announces to us that one of the main characters, the astronomer who is in love with the female protagonist, will end up dying by his own hand before he reaches the pinnacle of his career. Much later, toward the end of the book, the narrator lets fall that an extremely minor character, a doctor who appears in one brief scene, will die three months later in an air crash. It is not until the final page of the book that we understand how these facts come together and why we needed to know them, but in the meantime we have undergone a great deal of anxiety wondering which possible betrayals and discoveries (and there are several) could cause the astronomer to kill himself. Only at the end do we learn that all of our anxious guesses were wrong: the true course of events, as so often in life, turns out to be one we didn't expect.

To watch the predetermined plot unfold, like a recurrent nightmare that we are powerless to alter or avert, is a rich and compelling experience for a certain kind of reader. What is anxiety-provoking in nightmares—the arrival of the inevitable—becomes its exact opposite in a book, where knowing what is about to happen makes one more attentive, more alert, more open to the moment-by-moment texture of the experience. This is why I frequently reread both Patricia Highsmith and Henry James. This is why I take pleasure in the kind of narrative foreshadowing practiced by Richard Ford and Shirley Hazzard. And this is why we all read works whose plots we may well know in advance, like John Milton's *Paradise Lost*, David Malouf's *Ransom*, and Hilary Mantel's *Wolf Hall*.

Milton based his *Paradise Lost* on the familiar Garden of Eden story (though, granted, its familiarity to us now is at least partly thanks to Milton). In both the Bible and its Miltonic elaboration, the serpent tempts Eve and, through her, Adam to eat the forbidden fruit of knowledge, an act of disobedience that leads to humanity's ejection from eternal paradise. The book-length poem has now been around for so long that it seems natural for it to exist, but think how odd it must have been for Milton to undertake it in the first place. An epic retelling of a brief story from Genesis, couched in unrhymed iambic pentameters and intended to "justify the ways of God to men"—only a courageous madman, or an unconventional genius, would imagine he could accomplish such a thing. And yet it works, even three or four centuries later, and even for nonbelieving readers like William Empson and me. We may have to rejig the motive slightly, turning Satan into a heroic rebel and questioning God's degree of justification. We may feel unexpectedly moved and uplifted by the ending, which is supposed to be a tragedy of punishment, but which instead seems to view Adam and Eve's new life with something like hope, or even excitement:

> Some natural tears they dropped, but wiped them soon;
> The world was all before them, where to choose
> Their place of rest, and Providence their guide:
> They hand in hand with wand'ring steps and slow,
> Through Eden took their solitary way.

The common arguments about whether Milton intended us to feel this way—supportive, empathetic, almost optimistic about the possibilities open to the fallen mortals—are neither here nor there. It doesn't matter. The poem, leading us in its own direction, exists apart from its maker, just as Adam and Eve existed apart from theirs.

Nobody reads *Paradise Lost* for the plot, of course. But knowing what will happen lends an essential element to the experience of reading, in that it creates the exact tension between predestination and free will that Milton is attempting to explore in the poem. We know where these characters are headed and yet, minute by minute, we feel no sense of moral or epistemological superiority to them. On the contrary, we undergo their fates *with* them, as if in real time, or perhaps even a stretched-out version of real time, a version that mimics eternity. It takes forever for them to fall, and we hope for every moment of that forever that they will resist; then, when they have fallen, we hope they will get away with it. Our foreknowledge and our sympathies are completely at odds, just as God's would have been (or ought to have been, if he was a good God). If this mixed reaction on our part doesn't finally justify Him, it at any rate makes even His position more sympathetic.

A different kind of courage—somewhat less crazy and ambitious, but nonetheless intense—must have been required for the Australian writer David Malouf to produce his marvelous short novel *Ransom*, based on an episode from the *Iliad*. For writers, Homer is almost as much of a god as God, and to tinker with his perfect stories requires hubris of a notable degree. James Joyce possessed that hubris in grandiose form, and we can feel it exercising its assertive presence all the way through *Ulysses*. But *Ransom* (which understands that it comes not only after the *Iliad*, but also after *Ulysses* and Moravia's *Contempt* and all the other twentieth-century works based on Homer) is almost the opposite kind of work. It is small, and delicate, and intellectually modest. It does not trumpet its substantial intelligence at us.

Ransom takes as its departure point the section of the *Iliad* in which King Priam goes forth from Troy to collect the body of his son Hector from Achilles, the Greek enemy who has slain him. Achilles has always been viewed as a great character, and centuries of writers, from Euripides to Shakespeare to the moderns, have built great roles around him. Priam has not; only Malouf has been alert enough to ferret out his inner life in this subtle way. What he does is to hinge the whole novel on the relationship between Priam and his cart driver, a man whose name the king can't even remember (he repeatedly miscalls him by the name of his former driver), but on whom he comes to depend completely and, one might say, lovingly. Through the sensible, tender behavior of the cart driver—who, like Priam, is also a bereft father—we come to sympathize with the grief and fear and uncertainty of the otherwise inaccessible king.

It does not matter, in reading *Ransom*, whether you already know the story from the *Iliad* or not. Either way, the novel will cast its spell over you, because what keeps you going is not the larger plot question (whether Priam will or will not get his son's body back), but the step-by-step psychological moments that lead to that outcome. And "outcome" is too thin a word, in any case, for what happens to the characters, and to us, by the end of Malouf's novel. The result is not everything; the process is part of the result. This is one of the key realizations that accrues to Priam in the course of his quest.

The same realization, though achieved through very different methods, dawns on us as we read Hilary Mantel's *Wolf Hall*, which is itself a work about achieving results. Mantel is a master of using history to create fiction: she does so to great effect in her excellent novel about the French Revolution, *A Place of Greater Safety*. But in contrast to that earlier book, which covers ground that is basically in the international public domain, this more recent novel deals with a passage of English history that is at once broadly familiar and completely obscure. Mantel focuses on the period from 1527 to 1535, when Henry VIII was figuring out how to dispose of his first wife, Katherine of Aragon, and marry Anne Boleyn; in order to do so, he ended up breaking Catholicism's hold on England and naming himself the head of the church.

Everything you think you know about these events turns out to be inadequate to the discoveries made by this fictional work. By centering the narrative on Thomas Cromwell—a blacksmith's son who rose to become one of the king's most powerful advisors, and whose great-grandnephew eventually became the Protector of England, Oliver Cromwell—Mantel gives us a whole new perspective on the era and its machinations. Cardinal Wolsey, with whom Cromwell got his start, becomes a much more complicated and appealing figure than usual, and Sir Thomas More becomes downright hateful: not at all the saintly martyr portrayed in *A Man for All Seasons* and in Catholic theology generally, but a ruthless, narrow-minded egotist who cannot imagine the possibility of his own error.

Mantel is a great hater, and part of that greatness lies in the subtlety and modulation of her hatred. When she shows us More being casually cruel to his long-suffering wife (he insults her in Latin, a language she doesn't know, while she serves dinner to his guests), we think we will never forgive this man. And yet at the end of the novel, when Cromwell repeatedly visits the imprisoned More in an effort to get him to capitulate to the king and save his own life, we find ourselves adopting the same grudging admiration that Cromwell feels toward this now pitiful figure. It is with More's execution, in fact, that the novel ends, even though much still lay ahead in both Thomas Cromwell's and King Henry the Eighth's careers.

This *in medias res* approach is an essential aspect of Mantel's technique. She expects us to know things: that the king eventually executed Anne Boleyn, for instance, who is shown here only as a powerfully intelligent, destiny-controlling figure; that his subsequent wife was Jane Seymour, who merely gets a few brief though pointed cameos in the novel; and that all the children of his first three wives (first Edward, then Mary, then Elizabeth) ruled England in turn, despite his efforts to cut the two girls out of the line of succession. All these events take place outside and after the novel we hold in our hands, and we can certainly read *Wolf Hall* without knowing about them, but the fictional story becomes much richer if we are acquainted with the historical one as well.

The triumph of Mantel's novel, though, lies in its portrayal of Thomas Cromwell—a triumph that is all the more surprising when you consider that most historians have presented him as the Lavrenty Beria or Heinrich Himmler of his era, the evil henchman responsible for implementing his employer's violent wishes. In Mantel's much more sympathetic account, we witness at close hand Cromwell's public and private political negotiations, his astute business methods, his intelligent, multilingual dealings with all sorts of Europeans. We live with him in his house, watch him hire and train his servants, and share his sorrow as his wife and then his daughters die of the plague. His poor and violent background, his self-made and sometimes self-obscuring character, make him by far the most appealing figure in the crowd of devious nobles surrounding Henry the Eighth. All of this, needless to say, depends heavily on the language Mantel has devised to present her tale—a language that is neither archaic nor modern, neither ironically remote nor fully enmeshed in events, neither abstract nor individually nuanced, but one that floats, impossibly, at an invisible point equally distant from all of these.

I finished the rather hefty *Wolf Hall* wishing it were twice as long as it is. Torn away from that sixteenth-century world, in which I had come to know the engaging, pragmatic Thomas Cromwell as if he were my own brother—as if he were *myself*—I found myself turning to any available sources to find out more about him. I read each new piece of information about Tudor England with fresh and sharpened eyes. I thought back to Shakespeare, and wondered how purposely he was embodying the problem undermining Queen Mary's sovereignty—the question of whether a marriage to a deceased brother's wife is a real marriage or not—when he wrote *Hamlet* under the reign of her antagonist and half sister,

Queen Elizabeth. I even found myself visiting the Frick Museum, gazing at length on the Holbein portraits of Sir Thomas More and Thomas Cromwell that are hanging on its walls. But none of this, however instructive, made up for my feeling of loss, of having been ejected from a world that I could no longer inhabit because the final doors had now closed on me.

One would think that a sequel would solve this problem, and so it was with particular eagerness that I picked up the next volume in Mantel's Cromwell trilogy. *Bring Up the Bodies* is a well-told tale, worth reading for its own merits, but it is not as good as *Wolf Hall*. This should not have surprised me. Time after time, having finished the marvelous first novel in a series—Arnold Bennett's *Clayhanger*, Rebecca West's *The Fountain Overflows*, L. P. Hartley's *The Shrimp and the Anemone*, Olivia Manning's *The Great Fortune*, Edward St. Aubyn's *Never Mind*, and many others, too numerous to list—I have rushed to the second and third volumes to gobble up more about the characters, only to find myself disappointed. This is never a learning experience: you cannot refrain from taking the next step, any more than you can refrain from watching the episode that comes after a cliffhanger on TV. But though your curiosity may be satisfied, your much-raised expectations of pleasure will not be. With a handful of exceptions (Richard Ford's Frank Bascombe novels and Anthony Trollope's Palliser series come to mind), the sequels to a great first novel are bound to be distinctly inferior. The characters have grown up, or reformed, or otherwise lost their edge. The tale-telling has become dutiful, perhaps even a bit weary.

To these standard problems, Hilary Mantel's *Bring Up the Bodies* adds a few of its own. The author is stuck with the fact that the later career of Thomas Cromwell is more sordid and

less engaging than his early struggles. Also, since the story of
Anne Boleyn is already more familiar to us than the rest of
the Henry the Eighth tale, Mantel has to cope with the reader's
own expectations about the plot. And the unusual style she
invented to transmit both historical distance and narrative
intimacy (in particular, the use of an undesignated "he" to
refer to Cromwell) has by now, perhaps, begun to strike us as
slightly mechanical. None of this means that the novel is actively bad; I don't think Mantel is capable of writing a bad
novel. But it almost makes me wish—against my own readerly
interests—that she had chosen to end her story in midstream,
leaving me with that terrific, inconsolable hunger.

One can derive this sense of longing from narrative artworks
that are not literature. I felt something very much like it after
I finished watching the television series *The Wire*. I also felt it
at the end of *The Best of Youth*, the six-hour Italian movie that
first showed on Italian television. Very few standard-length
movies are capable of creating this sensation of loss; it requires the Wagnerian length and the Dickensian intimacy of
television, I think. And most television is not good enough to
accomplish it. But when it does happen, as in these two cases,
you get something that has a kind of literary profundity.

Here, I suppose, is where the definition of "literature"
gets fuzzy. You could insist that it must depend on the written word. But even television shows—that is, *good* television
shows—begin as scripts. If those scripts need full performance
to bring them to life, well, so do most plays; and since we are
willing to count drama as literature, why not television as
well? Besides, it may be that the *written* word is not as essential as we think. Consider Homer, who had no written text at
all, but simply sang his verses to those assembled around him,

relying on them to memorize and transmit the poems. Or what about fairy tales? They may have been gathered together by the Brothers Grimm and the like, but they existed in orally disseminated form long before that. At what point in their history, if ever, do such works become literature?

Certainly there is a great deal of literature that partakes of fairy tale; or, to put it another way, fairy-tale elements manage to make their way into a number of highly respectable novels, stories, and plays. The marriage plot—that whole century-long tradition, extending from Jane Austen, who delighted in giving us the marriage, to Henry James, who delighted in withholding it—stems in part from the fairy tale of the princess and her multiple suitors (a tradition that Shakespeare also drew on, in the three-casket subplot of *The Merchant of Venice*). Other works of literature are clearly based on the prince's quest for an almost-impossible object, a plot which underlies not only Don Quixote's explicitly chivalric escapades, but also Julien Sorel's relentless pursuit of higher social status in Stendhal's *The Red and the Black*, or Marcel's interminable search for a satisfying love affair in Proust's *Remembrance of Things Past*. Then there is the story of the provincial tailor's or cobbler's son who makes good among the aristocracy in the big city, a version of which lies behind both Balzac's *Lost Illusions* (which propels its protagonist, Lucien, from a small French town to bustling Paris) and Trollope's *Phineas Finn* (which transfers its title character from rustic Ireland to a London career in Parliament). My own favorite incarnation of the fairy-tale plot involves the collection of devices or talents or provisions or skills that are handed to the hero at the beginning of his journey and must be used— we know not how, until they appear at precisely the right moment—before his story reaches its end. There is something extremely satisfying about this process, whether it be the use of the characters' unique talents in Frank Baum's *The Wizard of Oz*, or the application of objects saved from shipwreck in Defoe's *Robinson Crusoe* and Verne's *The Mysterious Island*, or the necessary collaboration of the individual police officers, each of whom has a special skill, in the ensemble casts of Fred Vargas's *policiers*. Part of the pleasure has to do with a sense of efficiency, of materials exactly allocated and completely used. Another part has to do with a sense of inevitability, the feeling that *someone* knew where we were headed all along, even if we and the characters did not.

There are novelistic plots that play on this sense of inevitability and then give it an extra twist at the end, as if to satisfy us by meeting our expectations and also by evading them. I'm thinking, in particular, of the wonderful nineteenth-century novel *The Maias*, by the Portuguese writer Eça de Queirós. The plot of the novel occupies practically the whole century, covering the lives of three generations of the wealthy and colorful Maia family, though centering on Carlos Maia, its youngest member. We get details about his upbringing on his grandfather's country estate; we see the rural lives of the villagers who surround him there as well as the more sophisticated lives of the young men he meets as a student. We follow their efforts to undertake various cultural, artistic, and political projects (including founding a magazine) in a way that seems typical of young people in that era and that class, and yet particularly Portuguese at the same time. Nineteenth-century Lisbon is rendered in all its tinseled glory as a provincial capital aping London or Paris, with its own silly aristocracy and its own conventional manners. All this is done with tenderness and wit, and the book would be worth reading purely as a portrait of a fascinating society that we Anglophones know little about.

But the heart of the story, the plotline that keeps us compulsively reading, lies in the love affair Carlos conducts with the woman of his dreams, a dark-eyed beauty who happens to be married to someone else. Those of us with an eye for melodrama can spot the resolution coming from afar: de Queirós drops sufficient hints along the way to suggest to his more alert readers that this beautiful young woman will turn out to be Carlos's long-lost and previously unknown sister. We anxiously await the tragedy that will result when Carlos himself finds out, assuming that the discovery will mark the book's disastrous denouement. That moment of revelation arrives, but it is not the end. The author surprises us by concluding his book with a leap into the future, allowing decades to pass and awarding his main character a distanced view of these calamitous events from the calm perspective of the century's end. Carlos has survived, as have his close friends, his capital city, and his country—all in altered form, of course, but recognizably connected with who they were in their callow youth. It is an astonishing feat of authorial wisdom, this replacement of the expected melodrama with a sense of wry nostalgia; it is as if we were expecting a painting in primary-colored acrylics and were instead handed a beautiful pastel with the most subtle gradations of hue. The shock to our system is bracing, and salutary. We too feel that we have survived something, and have moved onto a plane that is suspended slightly above normal life, where we are contemplative and amused but still capable of being interested in what goes on around us. This is old age at its best, I suppose, and de Queirós renders it perfectly.

Not all plots are required to reach this kind of conclusion, or for that matter any kind of conclusion at all. There are plots in which nothing, essentially, happens. (Most of Beckett falls into this category.) There are plots which consist largely of thoughts rendered into words—stream-of-consciousness novels like Virginia Woolf's *To the Lighthouse* and Thomas Bernhard's *The Loser*, but also mystery novels that specialize in showing the detective's lucubrations. Plot need not be profuse or busy. It can linger on a few memorable moments; it can be stark, or scarce, or minimal.

Yet when plot is largely absent, as it is, say, in certain *nouveaux romans* or imagistic poems, we tend to fill the gaps ourselves, with our own pattern-creating minds. For we are plotting creatures, we humans, and we like to be told a story that goes somewhere. We like to sense the connections between seemingly disparate events, even though we may recognize that real disparities rarely resolve so neatly. Life often foils us in this respect, with its coincidences and its dead ends. We turn to literature to remedy the loss, to impose some kind of meaningful order on the nonsequential. And good literature, like *The Maias*, meets us only halfway.

TWO

THE SPACE BETWEEN

There will always be a gap of some kind. It may be located in places as small as the sentence, or even the individual word; it may govern entire relationships—among characters, between character and author, between author and reader. It may be a purely metaphorical absence, or it may involve an actual cut or deletion. But it is always there.

Sometimes the severance, the gap, is built into the authorial strategy itself. Dickens is a master of this. His most memorable characters seem to possess detachable parts—salient characteristics which, in taking on a life of their own, come eventually to represent the whole personality. The less realistic these humorously exaggerated characters are, the more they are prone to demonstrating a single, representative quality that exists apart from themselves. Yet in some ways these distinctive habits, always practiced to excess, are the most realistic thing about these people, for it is precisely in their notable excrescences that we are likely to recognize ourselves. Hardly a year ever passes, for instance, without my recalling Mr. Dick, the pleasant, loony gentleman in *David Copperfield* who is sane on every subject save that of King Charles's head. Unfortunately, he simply can't keep his mind off this beheaded monarch's gruesome appendage; it *will* keep popping into his awareness, and into his voluminous writings, despite his best efforts to keep it out. You would be surprised how many people suffer from their own variety of a King Charles's head. I am always surprised when I see my versions of it (and I have a number of them) popping up and ruining my pages.

Detachability is the key element here, not only for Dickens's metaphor, but for literary practice in general. It is the space left in between—the gap between Charles's imagined body and his severed head, the sliver of reality separating me from Mr. Dick—that thrives intensely, and perhaps singularly, in literary works.

Sometimes the gap is imposed from the outside, by a force even stronger and more uncontrollable than the writer's own obsessions. One of the strangest aspects of Dostoyevsky's *Demons* is the fact that its most powerful and seemingly necessary episode—the chapter in which Stavrogin confesses to the crime that underlies all his behavior, the long-ago rape of a young girl who subsequently committed suicide—was cut by the censorious editors before the book's publication. That crucial chapter (which Dostoyevsky repeatedly fought to keep in, but with no success) disappeared from *Demons* for the rest of the author's life, and for many decades after; even now it survives only as an appendix in most editions. How could the novel have existed without it? How could anyone have begun to understand *Demons* or respond properly to it without this essential key? And yet people did. Literature is a remarkable thing, and so are its readers. Together, they manage to triumph over even the most severe amputations, or decapitations.

Poetry, as it turns out, works largely through severances of this kind. In a poem, the kind of connection that is usually essential to our understanding of what is happening has been purposely removed. A bridge that normally leads between two precipices has been chopped away, and we are left to jump across on our own. Character and plot, the two elements that in the novel help us locate ourselves, are more shadowy, less evident in poetry, becoming transformed at times into just the sound of a voice, or the remembrance of an event. And yet they are still there, even in the briefest of poems; they are part of what enables us to leap over those chasms.

Consider the opening lines of one of Gerard Manley Hopkins's most wrenching sonnets:

> No worst, there is none. Pitched past pitch of grief,
> More pangs will, schooled at forepangs, wilder wring.
> Comforter, where, where is your comforting?
> Mary, mother of us, where is your relief?

We ourselves are pitched immediately into a profound emotional darkness, the superlative version of a nonexistent negative, with that strange, extreme phrase "No worst, there is none." Yet even here, in this state of complete abandonment, we are somehow held, enclosed, located in a feeling if not in a precise place. And that, I think, is because we can sense the presence of the characters and the relationship between them: the idiosyncratic, pain-wracked speaker, and those absent others ("Comforter," "Mary") to whom he pleadingly, uselessly speaks.

The poem, in its very language, reenacts and alludes to the procedure by which it operates, that leap across an unbridged chasm which the poet is now requiring of us, just as his God is apparently requiring it, in a much more painful fashion, of him. The sonnet ends with the lines

> O the mind, mind has mountains; cliffs of fall
> Frightful, sheer, no-man-fathomed. Hold them cheap
> May who ne'er hung there. Nor does long our small
> Durance deal with that steep or deep. Here! creep,

Wretch, under a comfort serves in a whirlwind: all
Life death does end and each day dies with sleep.

What has been cut out is not just the connective words (a comfort *that* serves in a whirlwind, may *those* who never hung there) or even letters (so that the arcanely poetic "ne'er" here has a radical, rejuvenated, bridge-chopped-off function). The fulcrum of it all, the platform from which speech emerges, has itself been eliminated. That steep or deep *what*? Where, in all this nothingness, can one locate that exclamatory Here? Yet despite the radical excisions, the voice is stronger than ever. Its rhymes are insistent to the point of comedy (though certainly no one is laughing here), and there is a tenderness in that appositive command—"creep, / Wretch, under a comfort . . ."—that brings a distinctly human note to this otherwise stark landscape. This is a voice that is continuing to speak even though no one is listening. And one senses that the person being addressed has changed by the end of the sonnet: no longer God or Mary, the presumed listener is now that wretch who can only find comfort in the thought of death. Hopkins may be speaking to himself here—*must* be speaking to himself, or we wouldn't feel so much agony emanating from the poem—but the poor, abandoned creature he is addressing is also his reader. This is our problem too, even if we don't know it yet. We are the other character brought to life by such a poem.

At its root, almost all lyric poetry is a conversation between a speaker and a listener—a one-sided conversation, to be sure, but still a dialogue of sorts, in which the feelings and expectations of the silent partner are taken into account. Generally the "I" is the poet and the "you" is the reader, but in some poems these pronouns represent fictional characters, as they might in a novel or a short story. Ezra Pound's "The River-

Merchant's Wife: A Letter," for instance, is very like a brief epistolary novel. Its "I" is a young wife writing to her husband when he is away, expressing her longing for his return and recalling the history of their marriage. "At fourteen I married My Lord you," Pound has her say, in his purposely stilted translation of Li Po's classical Chinese masterpiece. The stiltedness is no doubt meant to suggest the cultural distance between her and us (we who are the hidden, unspoken "you" of this poem, just as her husband is the explicit, spoken one), but it also conveys the shyness of a child bride in an arranged marriage who has come to feel more love than she ever expected to. And she takes pleasure in the fact that her husband is in love with her, too: "You dragged your feet when you went out," she recalls about the beginning of his trip. The emotion she expresses in this letter is both intense and suppressed; more is implied than is stated directly, and that too intensifies the feeling, or at least our response to it.

> If you are coming down through the narrows of the river Kiang,
> Please let me know beforehand,
> And I will come out to meet you
>   As far as Cho-fu-Sa.

she says at the end of her letter, and it is the longing expressed in the line breaks and word rhythms, as much as her explicit willingness to move toward him, that signals to us how powerfully she misses him.

Robert Browning's "My Last Duchess" is based on an equally fictional premise, but in this case the "I" is a wife-murdering duke and the "you" a visiting emissary from a potential new father-in-law. Nothing could be further in tone from the Pound. The obliqueness is there, yes, but it is of the villainously mustache-twirling, heavily ironic variety, and the suppressed emotion is not love but rage, or vanity, or petty annoyance. This poem is a scene from a play rather than an epistolary novel: the two characters occupy the same well-furnished set, sitting in a room of the duke's palace before a portrait of his late wife as he elaborates on his grievances and his solution to them.

> Sir, 'twas all one! My favour at her breast,
> The dropping of the daylight in the West,
> The bough of cherries some officious fool
> Broke in the orchard for her . . .
>   . . . as if she ranked
> My gift of a nine-hundred-years-old name
> With anybody's gift . . .
>   . . . Oh sir, she smiled, no doubt,
> Whene'er I passed her; but who passed without
> Much the same smile? This grew; I gave commands;
> Then all smiles stopped together. There she stands
> As if alive. Will't please you rise? . . .

The humor of this poem—and it has a great deal of Ripley-like humor, though also, as in Highsmith, a significant aura of threat—lies primarily in our wondering how the silent visitor is taking all this. Does he understand what the duke is telling him, and will this awareness prevent the marriage between "The Count your master's . . . fair daughter" and the emissary's garrulous host? Does the duke even care that this might be the result of his sly confession, or is he too proud (or too crazy) to realize that his words could have this effect? The brief drama is over before we get any answers to questions like these. All the pleasure of the piece lies in the unfolding of the duke's outrageous personality. He is the real character here; the duchess, though she claims the title and most of the poem, remains constricted by the unreliable narrator who describes her, and the "you," however courteously addressed, is merely a cipher, a prop used to evoke the story.

The second-person pronoun of a poem is always, by definition, a less substantial person than the first. Even when the
characters are not fictional—or perhaps especially in that
case—the "I" is the person best known to the poet, most
readily seen from the inside, most fully understood. (Though
I do not want to suggest that "seen from the inside" and
"fully understood" necessarily go together: sometimes, as in
a stream-of-consciousness rendering of a character's thoughts,
or a mad killer's perspective at the beginning of a murder
mystery, to be thrust inside is precisely *not* to understand.) The
poet's "I" is likely to be less distinct from the poet's real-life
self than the first-person narrator of most novels; it is more
like the "I" of an essayist, though it is not exactly that either.
Except in the cases where the setting is explicitly fictional, as
in the Pound and Browning poems, we tend to assume that the
poet is speaking to us directly. And this in turn means that
the "you" is meant to be us, even if the poet—because she is
either long dead, or far away, or a recluse, or simply a complete
stranger to us—cannot possibly have any idea who we really
are. The poem works because she *seems* to know us, seems to
have forged some kind of real connection with us.

> I'm Nobody! Who are you?
> Are you—Nobody—too?
> Then there's a pair of us!
> Don't tell! they'd advertise—you know!

Emily Dickinson's rendering of the poet-reader situation is
perhaps the sharpest and wittiest imaginable. Yes, we are nobody to each other, we who meet only on the page. But
that very invisibility makes "a pair of us": in that sense, we
are joined together (on the page if nowhere else) to the exclusion of all the rest. Dickinson's "Don't tell!" has a special
force, coming as it does from a poet who largely renounced

publication in her lifetime—but of course the silent "you" of
any poem is not in much of a position to tell, so this plea is
also a joke between us.

The dreamlike power of Dickinson's voice—she is there,
right inside us, and if she is a bit cracked, then so are we—
is unlike anything else in poetry. But something of that
boundary-crossing, that wish to overcome the gap between
first-person speaker and second-person listener, appears even
in poets who took a far more public stance. It is there in the
work of Walt Whitman (who managed to be both cracked
and public), and it is there even in the seemingly platitudinous
but secretly dark verse of Robert Frost. His excessively an-
thologized "Birches" begins with the observations of the poet
himself ("When I see birches bend to left and right"), but has
moved by the fifth line to an actual, other second-person
viewer ("Often you must have seen them") and then, a few
lines later, to a generic "you" who merges self and others, the
speaker and everyone else ("Such heaps of broken glass to
sweep away / You'd think the inner dome of heaven had
fallen"). A much weirder version of this grammatical shift
occurs in his little poem "The Pasture," which starts:

> I'm going out to clean the pasture spring;
> I'll only stop to rake the leaves away
> (And wait to watch the water clear, I may):
> I sha'n't be gone long.—You come too.

This may sound coy at first reading, but the more you read the
poem (which contains only one more stanza, also ending with
the same three-word refrain), the more you come to believe in
that "You come too" as a serious offer. A writer-farmer of my
acquaintance, a man who first encountered this poem as a
teenager, often thinks of those lines as he walks out into his

own pastures—sees himself as somehow accepting that invitation. How strange and yet how natural it seems, the fact that Frost, long dead, has now become an intangible "I," while the once-ghostly "you" has turned into a solid person moving through space. No matter: there's still a pair of them.

These two characters, "you" and "I," also inhabit the world of nonfiction literature. Our tendency is to take them at face value there—to believe, for example, that the essayistic, reportorial, journalistic narrator is the real thing in a way that the voice of a poem or the protagonist of a novel is not. But the reverse could well be the case. As Janet Malcolm has pointed out, "In a work of nonfiction we never know the truth of what happened. The ideal of unmediated reporting is regularly achieved only in fiction, where the writer faithfully reports on what is going on in his imagination." In other words, the author of imaginative literature presumably knows everything there is to know about her characters (or, if she does not, then who is to contradict her, for no one at any rate knows more). But with essays or journalism or autobiography, much necessarily remains unknown to the author, who is essentially constructing characters out of what he can grab as reality flings it past him. The fictional character *is* herself; the essayistic character is only a Platonic shadow, flickeringly cast upon the page, of a reality that fully exists elsewhere. And nowhere is this more true than in the case of the essayist's "I."

The doubt that the nonfiction writer instills in us is central to his enterprise. He makes us depend on that friendly fellow who engagingly tells us his life story or recounts an interesting set of events or observations, and then he undercuts that dependence by making us suspicious of his veracity. This suspicion is not an unfortunate by-product of his effort;

it needs to be there for the nonfiction piece to work. If the author neglects to alert us to a sense of his own unreliability, we may discover it on our own, bringing the whole house of cards down in one swift blow. (This is what happens, I think, in the first-person accounts of extremely narcissistic writers like Emma Goldman and Anaïs Nin, who believe too strongly in their own perspectives. Because they are incapable of doubting themselves, we do the doubting for them, and it ends by ruining their books.) But the balancing act required of such an author is a delicate one, for the suspicions can't be so strong as to undercut our dependence. We need to recognize doubt, but then we must somehow be encouraged to take the leap of faith that gets us to the other side of this chasm. If we end up in the abyss, the nonfiction writer has failed; if we remain stolidly on the safe side of the broken bridge, he has also failed. He needs to get us across, but with full foreknowledge of the dangers involved. It is both a trick and not a trick.

J. R. Ackerley, one of the most appealing nonfiction writers of the twentieth century, wrote in the brief foreword to *My Father and Myself*:

> The apparently haphazard chronology of this memoir may need excuse. The excuse, I fear, is Art. It contains a number of surprises, perhaps I may call them shocks, which, as history, came to me rather bunched up towards the end of the story. Artistically shocks should never be bunched, they need spacing for maximum individual effect. To afford them this I could not tell my story straightforwardly and have therefore disregarded chronology and adopted the method of ploughing to and fro over my father's life and my own, turning up a little more sub-soil each time as the plough turned.

By confessing this at the beginning, Ackerley both hands us our doubts and assuages them. Would we have noticed the problem on our own? Perhaps not. But now we are convinced that despite his desire to tell us a good tale, his willingness to tinker with history to keep us engaged, this author is bent on conveying the truth to us.

The confession need not be explicit to be effective. In Tobias Wolff's memoir *This Boy's Life*, the main thing we learn about the youthful Toby is what a liar he is. He lies to protect himself from his brutal stepfather, Dwight, but he also lies repeatedly to various other authority figures, like schoolteachers and police officers. What is to keep us from feeling that he is lying to us as well? Nothing—especially since there seems to be an insuperable gap between the boy this story is about, this terrible student who can't even graduate from a public high school, and the man who is constructing the elegant, persuasive sentences that tell us the story of the boy he once was. That is the gap Wolff must get us to leap over if we are to believe he is telling us the truth. Some of us may do it unconsciously, and that is fine. If you give this book to a thirteen-year-old boy, especially one who has had a troubling stepfather, he will take it into his room and not emerge until he has finished it. He does not care about authorial doubt; he cares only, for the moment, about the great, well-told story. But as one reads and rereads the book over the years (and as future generations read it, detached from its original context), it will become apparent that the story would not succeed without strenuously demanding of us that leap of faith.

In my own life, the nonfiction author who has most powerfully persuaded me both to believe him and to doubt him is George Orwell. When I first read the essays, I was like that thirteen-year-old boy: I was smitten, and I believed every word. Later, I came to feel that Orwell was lying to me— that he was relying too heavily on something like Ackerley's capitalized "Art," that he was constructing a self which bore no relation to any real person called George Orwell or even

Eric Blair. (The fact that he had adopted a pseudonym was part of the evidence against him, in my most accusatory phase.) Only lately have I come to see that the doubt is a necessary part of the belief, and that Orwell need no more be the "I" of his sentences than I need to be the "you" in order for the sentences to carry their ethical weight. In fact, Orwell's "you" *is* his "I." To the extent I imagined myself spoken to personally by him, I was mistaken. If we merged on the page (as Emily Dickinson and her imagined reader did), it was not because he became me, but because he insisted that I transform myself into him. This was not at all bad for me. I tend in any case to have an excessive sense of self, and it was good for me to be changed, even if only temporarily, into a grumpy, clear-eyed British socialist of the 1930s. It may have been a rhetorical device, but it was a device that I still believe is grounded in certain truths—the ones about class and identity and moral obligation, for example, that Orwell points out so tellingly in *The Road to Wigan Pier*, where he observes how "humiliating" it can be to watch coal miners at work:

> It raises in you a momentary doubt about your own status as an "intellectual" and a superior person generally. For it is brought home to you, at least while you are watching, that it is only because miners sweat their guts out that superior persons can remain superior. You and I and the editor of the *Times Lit. Supp.*, and the Nancy poets and the Archbishop of Canterbury and Comrade X, author of *Marxism for Infants*—all of us *really* owe the comparative decency of our lives to poor drudges underground, blackened to the eyes, with their throats full of coal dust, driving their shovels forward with arms and belly muscles of steel.

I may resist that "you" (as in other phases of my life I have resisted the casually homophobic insult to the "Nancy" poets, or the sentimental characterization of "superior persons" versus "poor drudges"), but the resistance is essential to Orwell's method. It is part of what will make these beautifully paced sentences continue to ring true even after there are no more coal miners left in the world.

If the second-person pronoun is a central character in Orwell's essays, it is one that is nearly absent from Montaigne's. This has much to do with their very different aims. Orwell, who was self-consciously refining the essay form for use as a publicly deployable weapon, was focused on the presence of an audience. Montaigne, who was inventing the essay essentially from whole cloth as a way of exploring his own personality and his own ideas, wrote for nobody but himself—or, if he wrote for anyone else, it was for a dead best friend who would never read his words. The world of Montaigne's essays is a severely enclosed one, and it can seem airless in comparison to Orwell's. It is not an easy place in which to spend time; its only character (aside from a host of distant and long-dead authors from whom Montaigne is constantly quoting) is that sole and perennial "I." But this limitation is not a shortcoming. It gives Montaigne the capacity to speak about things that Orwell and other conversational authors could not. Death, for instance, as he does here, in the late essay "On vanity":

> Not from fear but from cunning, I want to go to earth like a rabbit and steal off as I pass away. It is not my intention to test or to display my constancy during that action. For whom would it be? Then all my right to reputation and all my concern for it will be at an end. I am satisfied with a death which will withdraw into itself, a calm and lonely one, entirely my own, in keeping with my life—retiring and private . . . I have enough to do without having to console others; enough thoughts in my mind without fresh ones evoked by my surroundings; enough to think about without drawing on others. This event is not one of our social engagements; it is a scene with one character.

Montaigne's seemingly personal observation doesn't claim to be the last word on death—nothing could be that, after all—but the strength of this passage is nonetheless profound. Its charm and its astuteness both stem from the same curious tonal mixture of overt selfishness and secret companionableness. His own life, his own writing, may be particularly solitary, but in death we are all, finally, alone: that is why Montaigne, as a self-professed isolate, can serve as such an apt guide to this experience that none of us will ever fully have. Yet even to put it in this bald, imploring way is to subtract from the delicate irony with which he treats the untreatable. "This event is not one of our social engagements; it is a scene with one character." How is it that he can suggest the idea of theater and in the same gesture take it away, so that all thoughts of audience, of pretense, of a public of any kind, are banished from that scene?

Death may lower the final curtain on life, but it does not necessarily have the same effect in literature. This is yet another version of the space between: that liminal space which, in literature alone, marks the uncertain borderline between the dead and the living. Unlike the people who surround us in our daily existence, the characters in a literary work can continue to speak their minds to us from beyond the grave. (We may imagine that we can similarly hear from our own beloved dead, in dreams or hallucinations or simple remembrances, but these are *our* minds speaking to us, not theirs.) A literary character can be both dead and conscious; both dead and perceptive; both dead and reflective. A dead author can be this too, but not quite in the same way. Reading Henry James, who died thirty-six years before I was born (*only* thirty-six, I am amazed to realize, given that I once considered it another era—but he and I are growing closer and closer as I grow older and he stands still), I hear a voice that continues to speak its mind to me, making jokes I still find funny and psychological observations I still assent to. But even I, besotted as I am with this author, understand that he wrote these sentences as a living person, basically the same kind of living person that I am now. Whereas for those of his characters who incline toward the supernatural—the narrator of "The Jolly Corner," who returns to his long-ago home and meets his alternate self; the famous author in "The Private Life," who carries on an active social life while his double sits writing in the upstairs study; the governess in *The Turn of the Screw*, who imagines her charges have been invaded by morally evil ghosts—the border between life and afterlife is much more permeable.

This is actually less true of James than it is of certain other writers, because his best work deals with how those left behind feel about the departed, and not vice versa. He is essentially a chronicler of the regretful living and not the regretful dead. To attend closely to the latter, we need to turn to someone like Javier Marías, a Spanish writer whose "When I Was Mortal" (the title story of his first collection to appear in English) ably conveys this aspect of his fiction. The dead who watch the living, and long for them still, and wish to be back in that space where time passed, and mattered, and took its toll: this is the explicit subject of a few works by Marías and the implicit subject of many. "I often used to pretend I believed in ghosts," the narrator of "When I Was Mortal" starts by telling us, "and I did so blithely, but now that I am myself a ghost, I understand why, traditionally, they are depicted as mournful creatures who stubbornly return to the places they knew when they were mortal. For they do return." Javier Marías has a special feeling for these people who are no longer people; they preoccupy him, and he sympathizes with them to an unusual extent. This was apparent to me not only from his writing, but also on the one occasion I saw him speak at a public event. "Can you tell us something about the role of magicians, or seers, or tricksters, or ghosts in works of literature—specifically, your works of literature?" the onstage interlocutor asked him. "I choose ghosts," Marías answered, in English that was expressively perfect but not quite idiomatic, before going on to articulate the connection, at least in his own mind, between authorship and the dead.

Javier Marías is still very much alive, but something additional happens to such ghost-ridden works when their author himself dies. I used to listen to Thom Gunn read aloud his poem "Death's Door," in which he imagined how

> After their processing, the dead
> Sit down in groups and watch TV,
> In which they must be interested,
> For on it they see you and me.

Something of Thom's endearing wit steadily infused this dark poem, in which he imagined four of his friends—strangers in life, but dead in the same month—watching the black-and-white set together and gradually losing interest, until "snow blurs the picture" and they are "weaned from memory," loosed into the timelessness of the archaic dead. And I can still hear Thom's wit when I reread this poem to myself. But the voice in which it was conveyed is fading now, for he too has joined the dead and been swallowed up in that snow.

Emily Dickinson's voice has always had this quality of coming from beyond the grave—certainly for me, but perhaps even for her near-contemporaries, since so much of her work was only published after her death. "'Twas just this time, last year, I died," she begins one poem, in a rather

Rebecca-ish, *Sunset Boulevard*-ish vein (though it was Holly-
wood that stole from Dickinson, of course, not she who copied
from them). "I died for Beauty—but was scarce / Adjusted in
the Tomb / When One who died for Truth, was lain / In an
adjoining Room—" is the start of another of her precociously
posthumous poems. But the one I have always loved best opens
with the line "I heard a Fly buzz—when I died" and ends:

> I willed my Keepsakes—Signed away
> What portion of me be
> Assignable—and then it was
> There interposed a Fly—
>
> With Blue—uncertain stumbling Buzz—
> Between the light—and me—
> And then the Windows failed—and then
> I could not see to see—

It is the blueness of that fly's buzz, its absolute rightness and
specificity, that makes the verse so persuasive. She knows
what she's talking about, and the fly is the proof.

As further evidence from the land of the non-living, let
me call on another fly. This one appears in Ackerley's *My Father
and Myself*, when he is talking about the deathward decline of
his mother. "Ending up as I am with animals and alcohol," he
says, in what is surely one of the great throwaway clauses of all
time,

> one of her last friends, when she was losing her faculties,
> was a fly, which I never saw but which she talked about a
> good deal and also talked to. With large melancholy yellow
> eyes and long lashes it inhabited the bathroom; she made a
> little joke of it but was serious enough to take in crumbs of
> bread every morning to feed it, scattering them along the
> wooden rim of the bath as she lay in it . . .

Ackerley never hints that his failure to see the fly might cast doubt on its existence; if anything, he suggests the opposite, describing its physical features in microscopic detail. This fly's "large melancholy yellow eyes" make it as tangible as Dickinson's blue buzzer—and who is to say, at this late date, how real or unreal either fly was? They reside permanently, now, in the same landscape as Henry James's, Javier Marías's, and Thom Gunn's ghosts.

The uncanny in literature is not a separate place, reserved for those who believe in the occult or the supernatural. It is there in every poem that joins us to an absent speaker, every novel that sets up a parallel between our world and its world, every essay that calls to us from the distant era of a now-dead author. That eerily bridgeable gap between the you and the me of a literary work is also a space between the living and the dead, the imagined and the real, the singular and the collective. Even the very word "space" is doing double duty here, for it points to something that is both there and not there: it is the placeholder that joins us in a sequence (like the single space between each of these words) and it is the severance, the emptiness, that keeps us apart. Like all such ambiguous connectors, it is invisible to the casual glance, but we would know instantly if it were to disappear, for in that case the sentence, the stanza, the entire literary structure, would disintegrate on the spot.

THREE

NOVELTY

There is a certain kind of writer who seems to feel that unless he is breaking apart everything that came before him, composing something that in his own view is astonishingly new, he is not writing great literature. Though he is sincere in his wish to be a great writer (and in that sense might seem almost naive), his preferred mode of public address is sarcasm or heavy irony, both of which are meant to suggest his sophistication, his superiority to banal questions about reality, authenticity, and truth. He has no interest in accurately representing human behavior, partly because he has no interest in accuracy and partly because he has very little interest in other people; what concerns him most is the working of his own mind. He hates with a passion the realist novelists and formalist poets who came just before him, and he is convinced that only he, among all the writers who ever lived, is producing work that will matter to the future. In this respect, he evidently imagines a future filled with people who are nothing like him—people who will be content to rest with the innovations he has produced and will not feel obliged to stomp on their forebears.

Writers like this have given novelty a bad name. They

have led those who are wedded to old-fashioned notions of plot and character to conclude that innovations in style or structure are antagonistic to these older values, as if we could only have one of the two aspects—let us call them startling originality and enduring sympathetic gratification—so we have to choose between them. This obsessive clinging to the cherished ways of the past is almost as bad as its opposite. It is equally humorless, equally self-enclosed, and equally unlikely to lead to the production and enjoyment of great literature. I have no prescriptions for producing great works, but I have enjoyed a vast number of them, and from this outsider's perspective I can pretty confidently say that what is entailed has an element of openness to it. Rigid rules of any kind will be of no use here. Nor will the overweening desire to achieve newness, on the one hand, or protect tradition, on the other, because both of those positions imply a goal that is separate from, and often detrimental to, the more intrinsic purpose of simply telling the truth as one sees it. I say "simply," but it is not at all a simple matter. Literature that tells lies is not worth the paper it is written on, but a lie is not the same as a fantasy, an invention, an allegory, a myth, a dream. Fiction, drama, poetry, and even essays can be made up and also truthful.

Usefully for my purposes, one of the works of literature which most strongly expresses this complicated view is also one of the most innovative in form. I am referring to Miguel de Cervantes's *Don Quixote*—perhaps the most stylistically ambitious novel ever undertaken, in no small part because it was one of the first. What does it mean for an author to get inside his characters' minds and relay their thoughts, rather than simply displaying their actions on a theatrical stage? What is a "narrator," and how does he connect with the author of a work? How do the realities of fictional characters' lives compare to the realities of readers' lives, and where, if anywhere, do the two planes intersect? Does the book exist in its own time or in the time when you are reading it, and does that mean it exists in a different way for each new reader? Can the reader himself inhabit more than one era, time-traveling through books? Can the past, in this sense, be made to live again, and if so, can the nonexistent, purely fictional past also be brought to life? Are dead authors different from living ones, from a reader's point of view? How do poetry, drama, history, and fiction overlap? What is novel about the novel?

Cervantes was possibly the first person to ask most of these questions, and probably the first person to answer them—not flatly or pedantically, but with hints, suggestions, jokes, and intimations, through novelistic strategies that honored plot and character even as they worried about the existence of such things. There is no ancestor-stomping in *Don Quixote*, in part because the book had no immediate ancestors: it was *sui generis*, emerging from Cervantes's brow like Athena from Zeus's, whole and perfect.

The tone is sardonic but also genial, at once sharp, critical, empathetic, and companionable. The hero—a devoted reader, just like us—is the most lovable madman imaginable. (Dostoyevsky's Prince Myshkin perhaps runs a close second, as he was intended to do, for Dostoyevsky, despite the astonishing innovations he brought to the novel, was no enemy of the past: he deeply admired *Don Quixote*, and consciously borrowed from it for *The Idiot*.) The plot is a higgledy-piggledy series of adventures, to which we might be tempted to apply the word "plotless" if the whole book didn't so clearly and movingly lead up to its ending. That feeling which I mentioned in relation to *Wolf Hall*, of being summarily ejected from an enticing and richly detailed world, is Don Quixote's feeling when he recovers his sanity at the end of the novel.

It is also *our* feeling when we are finally forced to take leave of him.

One of the many things Cervantes discovered was that he could repeatedly remind his readers that they were reading a book—could, in that sense, blatantly announce the fictionality of his fictional characters—and still get us to invest emotionally in these people and their story. There are apparently at least two sides to our minds in such cases: one which goes logically about its business, registering Sancho Panza's jokes about typographical errors in previously published volumes of the knight's adventures as patent admissions of the story's fabrication; and another which takes Sancho, his master, and all the other characters at face value, allowing us to treat them as fellow humans, to laugh approvingly at Sancho's earthy wisdom, to weep wholeheartedly at the Don's death. We know the difference between reality and fiction (we are not, in that respect, as mad as Don Quixote), but that does not prevent us from feeling real emotions for these fictional characters. If anything, the fact that they sometimes comment on their own unreality makes them seem *more* real, as if they were capable of viewing their circumstances from the same perspective we do.

Cervantes was not the first writer to discover this for himself. There are numerous examples of it in his near-contemporary Shakespeare. And if we go even further back, to the Middle English works of Geoffrey Chaucer, we can find an especially pure version of it—an easygoing, entirely comfortable readiness to acknowledge the related but different planes on which authors and characters dwell. To give but one example: Chaucer ends his extremely moving account of Troilus and Criseyde's doomed love affair (a more sympathetic account, I would argue, than even Shakespeare's version in *Troilus and Cressida*) with the words

> Go, litel bok, go litel myn tragedye . . .
> . . . And kis the steppes, where as thow seest pace
> Virgil, Ovid, Omer, Lucan, and Stace

as if sending his poem out into the world in this literary-ancestor-acknowledging manner won't endanger or contradict the felt reality of his tale. As indeed it does not. What you might think of as the Wizard of Oz syndrome, that moment when the great and powerful Oz reveals himself as the little man working the effects from behind the curtain, can apparently coexist quite nicely with our continuing belief in the magic that little man produces.

Shakespeare is even braver than Chaucer in invoking this paradox, for he sometimes has his characters *themselves* deliver the envoi. At the end of *The Tempest*, when Prospero is renouncing the sorcery that has enabled him to rule his island throughout the play—the magical powers that have in essence brought the play into being—he comes forward in his final speech and asks us for our applause without in any way breaking character. Even more riskily, in *Antony and Cleopatra*, the doomed, captured Cleopatra, formerly the rebellious queen of Egypt and the proud mistress of Antony's heart, deplores what she can already foresee as the result of her captivity: a future in which

> . . . quick comedians
> Extemporally will stage us, and present
> Our Alexandrian revels: Antony
> Shall be brought drunken forth, and I shall see
> Some squeaking Cleopatra boy my greatness
> I' th' posture of a whore.

In Shakespeare's own time, these lines would have been delivered by the boy actor playing the female part. In other

words, this actor had to criticize his own squeaking delivery
at the same time as he convinced the audience of the character's palpable existence. And the character, through her lines,
had to persuade us that this existence would in some ghostly
form extend forever—allowing her as well as us to "see" this
performance—even as its mortal version ended tragically,
and at her own hands, less than two pages later in the script.

Theater, the art form which gave us the very notion of
"suspension of disbelief," specializes in such moments of con-
tradiction. Real humans, just like us, are standing bodily before us onstage, representing actions and emotions that cry
out for our sympathy, our hatred, our anxiety, our laughter,
our distress. We do not really forget that they are actors, just
as we don't forget that the sets they occupy bear little or no
relationship to reality, or that the lines they speak have been
written for them by someone else. All these factors, far from
being detrimental by-products, are built into the effective-
ness of the theatrical form. As audience members, we are indeed in a suspended state, where real emotions about non-real
events can course through us. But what is being suspended is
not, precisely, disbelief. Logic, evidence, empirical truth: these
elements that make up scientific belief, or even juridical disbelief, do not enter into it. We are not, as audience members,
being asked to weigh in on the innocence or guilt, truthful-
ness or falsity, worthiness or unworthiness of the people we
see before us onstage—not, at any rate, in the same way we
would have to make such judgments in a courtroom. Our
relationship to stage actors and the characters they represent
is both more remote and less antagonistic than that. Precisely
because we are not a jury of their peers, we can do things for
them, and they for us, that would not be possible in our normal reality. For the two- or three-hour duration of their performance, we give them life; and they, in turn, allow us to

become pure vessels of feeling, afloat in a world that for the moment seems as real to us as one of our own dreams.

The theatrical work, in this sense, reinvents itself each time it is performed. However old the script may be, it impresses us with its newness, its aliveness to our own present circumstances, even as it confesses its embeddedness in the predetermined past. This is true, at any rate, of *good* theater. It all hinges on quality. And the same is true, though in a different way, if the literary work is a poem or a novel. What Chaucer succeeds in doing in *Troilus and Criseyde*—reminding us of the existence of his poetic ancestors and at the same time leaving us enthralled by the freshness of his verse tale—cannot be done by just anyone. Cervantes is not the only novelist who can call our attention to the book in our hands and still make it live for us, but he is the best of them. The level at which the trick is performed matters deeply. If it is good enough, it ceases to be deception. Formal ingenuity, practiced at this level, becomes almost transparent. Far from being an intrusion from the outside, the author's intervention in his tale comes to seem an essential part of that tale.

One of the ways twentieth-century authors developed to remind us of their existence was the use of the footnote. What began as a sort of pseudo-scholarly addendum in T. S. Eliot's "The Waste Land" had become, by the time of Nabokov's *Pale Fire*, a whole story in itself—an epic meant to rival and even eclipse the fragile literary work to which it was attached. After that came the essays and novels of David Foster Wallace, Nicholson Baker, Jonathan Lethem, and their many imitators, in which the footnote represented both a mimicry of academic style and a method of ironic self-commentary, so that to have second thoughts (and perhaps even third and fourth thoughts,

each appropriately numbered on the page) was a way of sig-
naling that *some* kind of thought was at any rate taking place.
The typography of the footnote—the fact that it came in a
different size from the regular type, often accompanied by
a number, and always with a placeholder embedded in and
noticeably interrupting the writing itself—appealed to these
novelty-seeking *litterateurs*, as did its placement on the bottom
of each page, usually with a thin half-line fencing it off from
the text above. By reminding readers of the actual print technology through which the writer was communicating with
them, these typographical oddities reinforced the sense that
some kind of veil was being pierced; at the same time, the
footnote offered opportunities for new veils, new masks and
disguises, new ways in which the author could seem to argue
with or undermine himself.

Yet this twentieth-century invention was not really new
at all. One has only to look back to Jonathan Swift's *A Tale of
a Tub*, composed in the late seventeenth century and first
published at the beginning of the eighteenth, to find a similar
game being played with footnotes. I do not recommend reading the whole of *A Tale of a Tub*: like many of its twentieth-
century descendants, it is so taken with the cleverness of its
form that it disregards the problem of readable content. But
the footnotes themselves can be a delight, as when Swift has
his anonymous editor comment on the anonymous text, "I
cannot guess the Author's meaning here, which I would be
very glad to know, because it seems to be of Importance."
Some of the notes are even embedded in little blank rectan-
gles in the text itself, a format which the twentieth-century
authors would surely have borrowed if they could, since it
interrupts the tale even more pointedly than the normal kind
of footnote.

You needn't read far into *A Tale of a Tub* to get the point.

In fact, the pinnacle of its self-undermining humor occurs a mere three or four pages into the text, where we are confronted with all the typographical elements battling together at once. A footnoting dagger-sign in the text is followed by four and a half lines of asterisks, amid which the words "Hiatus in MS." are inscribed in smaller italic type. The text then resumes as before; but if we follow the dagger to its twin below, we get the Editor's footnote:

> Here is pretended a Defect in the Manuscript, and this is very frequent with our Author, either when he thinks he cannot say any thing worth Reading, or when he has no mind to enter on the Subject, or when it is a Matter of little Moment, or perhaps to amuse his Reader (whereof he is frequently very fond) or lastly, with some Satyrical Intention.

This single footnote is, to my mind, the best thing about *A Tale of a Tub*, just as the best part of Swift's equally clever (and equally impenetrable) *Battel of the Books* lies in the first sentence of its preface, where the again anonymous author proposes to define satire for us. "Satyr," he says, "is a sort of Glass, wherein Beholders do generally discover every body's Face but their Own; which is the chief Reason for that kind Reception it meets in the world, and that so very few are offended with it." I think this comment goes a long way toward explaining why satiric authors like Don DeLillo and Thomas Pynchon were so loved by their late-twentieth-century audiences. It is not difficult to charm one's readers when one seems, by giving them the wink, to include them in the inner circle of those who know better. Great satire, to last, needs to be offensive even to those who agree with it.

"A Modest Proposal" is Swift's breathtaking achievement

in this genre. Even now, nearly four hundred years after its first appearance, to read it is to be taken aback. It starts calmly enough, with potentially disturbing ideas masked in scrupulously inoffensive prose:

> It is a melancholly Object to those, who walk through this great Town, or travel in the Country; when they see the *Streets*, the *Roads*, and *Cabbin-doors* crowded with *Beggars* of the Female Sex, followed by three, four, or six Children, *all in Rags* . . . I think it is agreed by all Parties, that this prodigious Number of Children in the Arms, or on the Backs, or at the *Heels* of their *Mothers*, and frequently of their *Fathers*, is *in the present deplorable State of the Kingdom*, a very great additional Grievance . . .

I think it is agreed: in that phrase lies the special brilliance of the voice that Swift has invented to put forth his little idea. A half-century before Adam Smith's "invisible hand" and a century before Jeremy Bentham's utilitarian doctrine, he has come up with the simple expedient of maximizing public good by eliminating any sentimental concern for the individual. It is all a matter of pounds, shillings, and pence: those who have money will buy the new product from those who do not, and everybody will measurably benefit all round. For "no Gentleman would repine to give Ten Shillings for the *Carcase of a good fat Child*; which, as I have said, will make four dishes of excellent nutritive Meat, when he hath only some particular Friend, or his own Family, to dine with him." Swift goes on to suggest that, when the market fully emerges, butchers will proliferate to handle these mothers'-milk-fed year-old offspring of the poor—"although I rather recommend buying the Children live, and dressing them hot from the Knife, as we do *roasting Pigs*."

You do not need to know anything about famine conditions in eighteenth-century Ireland or the political relations between the Irish and the English to find this little essay chilling (though that knowledge will certainly enrich your reading of certain lines). The voice speaks to us now, about *our* poverty, *our* wealth, *our* political championing of the national good, and *our* penchant to make welfare decisions in light of budgetary considerations. We are eating those babies still. And Swift is onto us: this is the writer-reader pact turned on its head, with all that cozy winking and mutual self-congratulation turned into something horrifying. What he invented, in "A Modest Proposal," was not just that fatuously self-satisfied narrative voice, but the whole idea of a counterfactual work of nonfiction. This is what I meant when I said earlier that even an essay could be made up and also truthful. Swift's essay is both, and we can still hear its gruesome honesty echoing down the corridor of four centuries.

One can't tell yet whether nonfiction novels like Truman Capote's *In Cold Blood* and Norman Mailer's *The Executioner's Song* will last as long. Probably not, since very little literature endures as well as "A Modest Proposal" has. But I do not mean to criticize Mailer and Capote on this account. Their efforts to create a new genre that fit their own time were both brave and compelling. It is probably no coincidence that these two books, like Swift's essay, dealt with the subject of murder, for that is a subject that habitually causes us to mingle lies with truths.

In Cold Blood came first chronologically, but it is *The Executioner's Song* that has, over time, stayed with me as the greater book. My profound affection for Mailer, which stretches beyond this single work and covers much of his nonfiction writing, is something I can't fully explain. I do not particularly care for war stories or boxing or Marilyn Monroe or ancient Egypt; I have little patience with masculine posturings about violence and sexual prowess. But there is something about Mailer's voice that I have always loved—not the voice of the fiction, which often strikes me as crude and undeveloped, but the sinuous, chatty, abrasive, self-mocking voice of the essays and nonfiction books. Mailer can be just as crazy in his nonfiction as he is in his fiction (witness his bizarre theories about cancer, or about the communal need for blood revenge), but in the memoirs, essays, and political accounts, that craziness is couched in a prose style that knows itself better than we can ever know it. A good Norman Mailer sentence is a complicated work of art that can be unpacked in many ways, but at its heart there is always a simple mechanism: a two-way mirror that allows the author to reflect on himself even as we peer in at him.

The odd thing about *The Executioner's Song* is that it manages to capture something of this reflective quality even though, for perhaps the first and only time in his nonfiction work, the author is utterly absent from its pages. In this case, the two-way mirror is there primarily for *our* benefit. If we are alert enough, we can see our avid, amoral selves reflected back at us even as we examine the ostensible subject: the murders committed in 1976 by Gary Gilmore, and the media circus that surrounded his execution. But this self-reflectiveness does not account for the full extent of the book's value, nor for its allure. What makes it succeed as a narrative work of art is that Mailer, aided by his enormous respect for reality and history, is able to create credible literary characters out of actual people. This is not as easy as you might think. Read just about any news story about a killing or a trial and you will see what I mean, for in most cases all we get—if that—is a

wisp or shred of character, a fleeting phrase or a single descriptive term. Only a novelist (as Janet Malcolm suggested)
can really know about the interior lives of his characters; the
nonfiction writers have to guess.

Malcolm happens to be one of the few writers whose
journalistic characters, like Mailer's, have the fullness of people
in a novel. Yet her authorial voice couldn't be more different
from his. Where Mailer is loud and heated, Malcolm is subdued and cool. If he bodily intrudes on almost every situation
he is observing—*The Executioner's Song* is the great exception,
in this regard—she tends instead to dwell in the shadows,
emerging only intermittently. (I suppose *Iphigenia in Forest Hills*
would be her equivalent exception, her single instance of plac-
ing herself onstage in the drama.)

I suspect I am drawn to them both for similar reasons,
which may well be connected to the fact that all three of us
are fascinated by murder stories. This preoccupation is not
quite the same as the one that causes millions of people to
consume mysteries (though I share that one, too). Mailer and
Malcolm feed a somewhat different level of curiosity. The
whodunnit aspect is relatively submerged in their work: we
might know who the killer is from the very beginning of
the story, or we might never find it out. Even the *why* remains relatively opaque, in a book like *The Executioner's Song*
or *The Journalist and the Murderer*, because part of the point of
each of these books is that we cannot hope to plumb the
causes and motivations behind extreme violence. The central
characters themselves, those characters who began as real
people, do not appear to understand fully why they have done
what they are accused of doing; they either cannot or will not
explain it to our satisfaction. And yet we have a desperate
desire to know.

That, among many other things, is what Malcolm's and

Mailer's books are about—our readerly desire to penetrate what Joseph Conrad, in *The Secret Agent*, wryly called the "impenetrable mystery . . . destined to hang for ever over this act of madness or despair." Conrad's wryness comes in large part from the fact that he is ostensibly quoting the overheated language of a newspaper account. (Another part of it, though, comes from the mere fact that he is Conrad: that kind of distance was always inherent in his worldview.) It is through newspapers that most of us get our first intimations of such murderous and self-murderous acts, so it should not be surprising that the news media themselves form a large part of the subject of both *The Journalist and the Murderer* and *The Executioner's Song*. Yet it *is* surprising, in that we have rarely witnessed it before. We have hardly ever seen the news-gathering telescope turned in both directions at once. That dual perspective, that capacity to look both outward and inward at once, is part of what makes Malcolm's and Mailer's works "novel" in both senses: new, and also fiction-like. The great authorial innovation, which is both structural and ethical, lies in turning the reflecting mirror back on the investigating press at the same time as the reader is forced to credit the discoveries of that flawed press—a category which includes, naturally, the author of the work in hand.

Something like that double-sided mirror also appears in the work of Roberto Bolaño, one of the few recent fiction writers who has been able to bridge the gap between overt formal invention and a steadfast investigation of human behavior. Bolaño, a Chilean novelist who died in 2003 at a very young but also very old fifty, was obviously a fan of the French surrealist poets and their often bizarre followers. In book after book, his characters club together to start literary movements whose main function appears to be to confound bourgeois expectations. As elements in the novels, we are offered meandering and incomplete plot summaries, digressive anecdotes that overwhelm their settings, ridiculous journal titles, cut-and-paste versions of poetry, and all manner of stylistic tics that cover the ground between piquant entertainment and purposeful tedium. Sometimes Bolaño's novels even partake of these experimental quirks as well as describing them. But always, underneath, lies a recognizable, morally astute, amused but serious narrative voice which cares about the fates of specific characters. This is as true of the unfinished *Woes of the True Policeman*—whose central figure, Amalfitano, is one of the most appealing characters in all of Bolaño's work—as it is of fully achieved novels like *Distant Star* and *By Night in Chile*. And indeed, the fact that his final novel remains unfinished does little to damage its emotional impact on us, for it is in the nature of Bolaño's fictional worlds that they trail off: incompletion is one aspect of their special kind of realism, just as our inability to know everything is one of the truths they leave us with.

If I had to name a single quality that makes Roberto Bolaño's fiction compelling, it would be his capacity for stringent, hard-nosed sympathy. This is not the same as universal empathy or divinely inspired forgiveness or any of that soft-headed nonsense. Bolaño is never blind to the crimes of humanity and of particular humans. They are, after all, his major subject. But he is able to create fictional works that enter equally into his own mind and the minds of others, even when those others are killers, or hypocrites, or madmen, or literary critics. It is not that he leaves behind notions of good and evil, but that he makes them seem inadequate as categories. There is a continuum that links his monsters and killers, on the one hand, and his writers and dreamers, on the

other—or rather, a mirror, with those on opposite sides
twinned in the reflective surface.

Overtly and covertly, the idea of twins and other paired
figures pervades Bolaño's universe. Sometimes he gives us
a fictional stand-in for himself, a character named Arturo
Belano. More often the narrator himself is a Bolaño-like figure who gets paired with someone else. At the end of *Distant
Star*, for instance—a short novel about a right-wing Chilean
killer named Carlos Wieder, in which twins, mirrorings, and
pairings have riddled the plot—the Bolaño-esque narrator is
sitting in a café in Catalonia, reading Bruno Schulz:

> Then Carlos Wieder came in and sat down by the front win-
> dow, three tables away. For a nauseating moment I could see
> myself almost joined to him, like a vile Siamese twin, look-
> ing over his shoulder at the book he had opened . . . He
> was staring at the sea and smoking and glancing at his book
> every now and then. Just like me, I realized with a fright,
> stubbing out my cigarette and trying to merge into the pages
> of my book.

"Sympathy" is too paltry and flaccid a word for the state
of mind this describes. It is a powerful and unwilled form
of identification, a Houdini-like vanishing act that allows
Bolaño to merge with his scariest and most repellent creations as much as with his likable ones.

Nowhere in his work is this strategy clearer than in *By
Night in Chile*, a short masterpiece published just three years
before his death. The whole novel is a rant, or contemplation,
or act of memory taking place in the mind of its main character, Father Urrutia Lacroix, also known as the literary critic
H. Ibacache (he is his own twin, in other words, like all the
other double-named villains in Bolaño's work). Now on his
deathbed, Father Urrutia is recalling his experiences as a

Chilean literary figure before and after the coup. He thinks back on an encounter with Pablo Neruda; he remembers various figures of the left and (mostly) right; and he recounts— not just once, but three times—his glimpsed or imagined vision of the basement torture chamber where an American agent interrogated suspects during his wife's literary salons. All of this is done in a vibrantly alive yet hushed voice that floats somewhere between willed stupidity and luminous knowledge, between self-communion and self-justification, between exhilaration and despair.

That there is indeed a hidden connection between despair and exhilaration is made explicit by a character in another novel, the female narrator of *Amulet*: "And when I heard the news it left me shrunken and shivering, but also amazed, because although it was bad news, without a doubt, the worst, it was also, in a way, exhilarating, as if reality were whispering in your ear: I can still do great things; I can still take you by surprise, silly girl, you and everyone else . . ." *Amulet*, which was written immediately before *By Night in Chile*, was like a dry run leading up to the greater work. Bolaño made two advances in the later novel: he put the narrative into the mouth of a dislikable character, and he eliminated himself entirely from the book. There is no Arturo Belano in *By Night in Chile*. There is no Bolaño figure of any kind, unless we count the "wizened young man" of whom the priest seems so afraid, but he could be anybody, including Death. In *By Night in Chile*, the author has finally done exactly what he feared so greatly in *Distant Star*: that is, merged bodily with his most despicable character. Without even the separateness of "vile Siamese twins," they have become a single person, a frightened and dying man living off the memories of his Chilean past, dreading the annihilation of himself and all his writings. There could be no character less like the real

Roberto Bolaño than Father Urrutia—a member of Opus Dei, a smarmy literary careerist, a right-wing snob, a religious hypocrite, a worm in the service of Pinochet. And yet for the duration of *By Night in Chile* we are horribly and, yes, exhilaratingly inside him.

It is rightly said of W. G. Sebald, a writer with whom Bolaño is sometimes compared, that all his characters are essentially versions of their author. This, I think, is a flaw in his novels, particularly *Austerlitz*, which purports to be about someone else. A similar flaw afflicts an even greater writer, Franz Kafka, whose strongest works are almost unbearable because of the airlessness of their self-enclosure. Roberto Bolaño is an author who risks exactly this charge and then triumphs over it. Finally, it is not that all his creations are projections of himself, but the opposite: in his novels, he becomes a mere figment of his characters' reality, a shadow in their dreams. Like the French surrealist poets he so admires, he carefully sets up the trick mirrors, constructs all the cunning aesthetic parallels, assures us that he is playing with us— and then smashes the whole construction to bits. When the dust clears, all that's left (but it is more than enough) is a moment of true feeling.

The desire to innovate is not what lies at the heart of books like these. If it were, they would feel much flimsier, morally and aesthetically, than they do. In each case, the author's primary aim is to reveal the truth, and the novelty of form is just a by-product of that aim. This is the paradox that lies behind formal inventiveness: you can only achieve an exemplary kind of novelty if it is not, primarily, what you are trying to achieve. As an end in itself, stylistic innovation is merely a way of showing off, a useless if mildly entertaining trapeze act; only when harnessed to the author's fervent truth-telling does it become significant.

To tell the truth in literature, each era, perhaps even each new writer, requires a new set of authorial skills with which to rivet the reader's attention. We are so good at lying to ourselves, at lapsing into passive acceptance, that mere transparency of meaning is insufficient. To absorb new and difficult truths, we need the jolt offered by a fresh style. Yet what is startling at first eventually hardens into either a mannerism or a tradition. Even Swift's "A Modest Proposal," if read too early and too often (in a classroom setting, say), can come to seem a mere example of Satire. So every writer—every *good* writer, every writer who really has something to say—must figure out for herself a new form in which to say it. The figuring need not be conscious, and the innovation need not be dramatic or obvious; we can be affected by style without necessarily perceiving the sources of the effects. But if we do perceive them, they cannot detract from our sense of the writer's seriousness (a seriousness that, in the case of an innovator like Mark Twain, may partake of a great deal of humor). The structural and stylistic eccentricities must seem—and be— essential, not merely ornamental.

Take *Moby-Dick*, for instance. Reading that novel (if it is indeed a novel, and at times I have my doubts), we do not say to ourselves, "Oh, that Melville is such a show-off." The informational chapters that interrupt the tale, the ones with titles like "Cetology" and "Of the Monstrous Pictures of Whales" and "Jonah Historically Regarded," do not strike us as expert research fetched up by the super-smart Melville from his vast library of whale knowledge. There is no Melville here. He has faded completely into his story, becoming "a nonentity, like Shakespeare," as William Carlos Williams astutely put it. The grandeur of *Moby-Dick* stems partly from the fact that it seems larger than any individual author—larger than the self-described Ishmael who is supposedly telling us the story, but also larger than the real author we know must lie behind him. (But we know it only with the purely rational side of our brains: we do not feel it, just as we do not feel Shakespeare pulling strings behind the stage, nor Milton directing Adam and Eve toward their predestined fates.) It may seem tedious at times to plow through the masses of information that punctuate Captain Ahab's quest for the great white whale, but eventually we come to realize that they *are* the story, just as much as the quest is. No clever game is being played with us, no puzzle is being presented for our ingenious and self-satisfying solution. We are simply being dropped into a new kind of reality, in which we will either sink or swim; by the end, perhaps, we may have learned to do both.

For a very different approach to literary innovation, consider James Joyce's *Ulysses*. This is a novel that has always gotten on my nerves. I admit that part of what is annoying is how much other people love it and praise it, when it leaves me completely cold. I vastly prefer the youthful author of *Dubliners*, and even the slightly pushier fellow behind *Portrait of the Artist as a Young Man*, to the highly self-conscious innovator who wrote *Ulysses*. By the time he reached that point, Joyce had begun to congeal into the artist who would eventually produce the nearly unreadable *Finnegans Wake*, and the obvious source of the rot was his overweening desire for a great literary reputation. This trumped all other literary desires on his part, so that things which had mattered to him earlier—the creation of believable human figures, the portrayal of a particular moment in Dublin's and Ireland's history, the use of language as an element in our common experience, the reliance on real as opposed to fabricated emotions—all gave way to this one enormous wish: to be the greatest, most impressive writer of his generation. This is not a literary impulse but a self-promotional one, and you can sense it in every chapter, almost every line, of *Ulysses*. We are meant to admire each *tour de force* for its cleverness and its brilliance. We are meant to recognize and applaud the skillful scene-by-scene parallels between the heroic Homeric tale and its reduced Dublin version, the chortlingly amusing imitations of other literary forms, the archetypal renderings of Jew and Catholic and man and woman. Woman! Don't get me started. If I hate anything more than the rest of the book, it's that ridiculously orgasmic Molly Bloom soliloquy with which Joyce concludes—a ventriloquist's dummy masquerading as a character. Reading her breathy Yeses, I can hear her all-too-evident author congratulating himself on his literary genius.

Finnegans Wake may be less hateful in part because it is more of a noble failure. Here the effort to charm the reader through a flamboyantly displayed intelligence has tipped over into something weirder, more willful, more insistent on having its own way to the exclusion of all else. This myopic intensity presents us with a more interesting project than the slyly clever *Ulysses*, but it is still too self-regarding to be convincing as literature. Authorial performance, rather than being simply the novel's primary method, has become its *raison d'être*: there are no characters to be violated, no readerly sympathies to be toyed with, no fake emotions to be evoked, because all these old-fashioned novelistic elements have been jettisoned in favor of the desire to speak in a new kind of language. As poetry, *Finnegans Wake* may have value. As a novel, it does not really work, and only the most sympathetic Joyceans (myself certainly not included) have managed to make it all the way through.

At least one of those sympathetic readers was a great writer himself, and his reading of *Finnegans Wake* influenced him so heavily that his own innovative work grew out of it. I could be speaking about Samuel Beckett (who worked for a time as Joyce's secretary and absorbed the influence at first hand), but in this case I'm actually referring to Thornton Wilder. His 1942 play *The Skin of Our Teeth* was a direct response to Joyce's late work—almost a borrowing from it, or a translation of it into understandable dramatic form. The play is indeed more coherent than Joyce's novel, but it too is gigantic in its aspirations, attempting to encompass the whole history of mankind, not to mention all the various functions of the theater, in its brief evening-length range. And it too now seems a bit of a noble failure, though it did win the Pulitzer Prize for its year.

The ironic fact is that Wilder had already created his most formally ingenious and original work a few years earlier, in a play that appears to have nothing whatsoever to do with Joyce, or indeed with any other piece of writing I've ever encountered. *Our Town*, like *Moby-Dick* and all other truly innovative works of literature, seems to have no direct ancestor but itself. Often disguised as a somewhat sentimental piece of Americana (particularly when it is performed at the grade-school and middle-school level, as it so often is), Wilder's play about Emily Webb, George Gibbs, and the other small-town inhabitants of Grover's Corners is actually a quietly radical piece of theater. I might never have realized this, had I not seen the revelatory production that was directed by David Cromer at the Barrow Street Theater in 2010. Assembled with the other onlookers who were seated on bleachers surrounding and even among the performers, I understood for the first time that we too are the ghostly presences to whom and of whom Emily is speaking in her final, after-death soliloquy; we too belong with the temporarily living characters who will someday be numbered among the dead. And Cromer, by taking on the role of the Stage Manager (the role that, in both its novelty and its down-to-earth practicality, most clearly pinpoints Wilder's revolutionary technique), actively helped me toward this realization. Delivering those perspective-shaping lines in his own flat, Midwestern, non-actorly voice, occasionally standing among and even touching the audience members as he spoke, David Cromer personally cemented the connection between the play's reality and our reality, for we knew that as the director he really *was* the play's stage manager.

A play is a form of literature that only completely exists onstage. That is merely its shadow, or its embryo, that we read in script form, and if one's theatrical expertise is insufficient, as mine certainly is, a script alone may fail to yield up some of the work's most important effects. It took Cromer's fully embodied version of *Our Town* to remind me of something I've had to rediscover repeatedly: that deep feelings are by no means incompatible with artistic self-consciousness. Both the human heart and the theatrical fourth wall were pierced by that singular performance, and the familiar paradox lay in the fact that my awareness of being in a theater space with other silently weeping audience members contributed to, rather than shattered, the illusion. And what *was* the illusion, exactly? That these characters were alive? (But they told us themselves they were long dead.) That human lives could be viewed from a distance, as if historically or even geologically? (But the play itself was allowing us to see things in that way.) Or perhaps that these quotidian tragedies—hope disappointed, early death, longing, regret—had some kind of bearing on our own lives? If that is an illusion, I wonder what reality might be.

•

The kind of magic Thornton Wilder accomplished through his Stage Manager—that intermediary between the characters and ourselves, that broker of their experience to us—has long been performed in a less explicit way by nondramatic writers. In a novel or a poem, the stage manager is language, and the challenge for the author is to use it in the way Wilder used his: as a screen between us and the characters that somehow intensifies rather than diminishes our sense of felt connection with these fictional people. The language needs to point to itself as a tangible medium and at the same time afford us the transparency of a window onto another life. It must get in the way and get out of the way, all at once. I can think of many remarkable works that accomplish this, starting with *Don Quixote* if not with Homer, but for now let me focus on two writers of my own era.

Louise Glück is a poet whose works have always depended primarily on the powerful presence of a speaking voice. Whether she is writing discrete lyric poems, as in *The Wild Iris*, or linked narrative poems, as in *Averno*, we feel addressed—almost buttonholed, in a Coleridgian sense—by that emphatic speaker who is conveying his or her feelings to us. This is not exactly dramatic monologue in Browning's terms: the voice is less personal than that, the character less specific. It is a voice that exists on the page alone and comes fully to life only when we are reading its words. The voice may have a backstory—often a complicated and rather disturbing backstory, in Glück's seriously intelligent and sometimes uncomfortable work—but it does not generally cohere into anything as specific as a biography. The episode, the encounter between us listeners and that Orphic speaker, seems to be complete in itself.

But in her recent volume *A Village Life*, the balance appears to have shifted slightly. The emphatic voice is still there, but it takes up residence in one person after another— one character after another, we would say if this were a novel. Yet *A Village Life* is not a novel, or even a collection of linked stories; it is very clearly a collection of separate but somehow related poems. What links the poems is not just geography, that undefined but apparently Mediterranean village in which all this speaking is taking place. It is also language, the European language (again undefined, but of a particular place and time) from which Glück seems to have translated all these speeches into English. It is an excellent, pure, almost transparent translation: there are no grammatical errors, nothing that is not perfectly idiomatic, perfectly in keeping with our everyday speech. And yet there is a sense of foreignness that hangs over the whole transaction. These voices, and the stories they tell us of their lives, are coming to us from elsewhere. The language is, in that sense, a barrier between us and the speakers, but it is also what conveys them so fully to us that we almost feel we are meeting them in person. And, as in *Our Town*, we sense that in meeting them we are also, in some obscure and indirect way, meeting ourselves. It is the distance, I suspect, that enables us to open ourselves to this feeling—we would be more guarded if the seemingly foreign language did not assure us that we had no self-scrutiny to fear.

A similar mechanism, though not the same one (for each author invents her own revolution, however quietly), governs the language of Penelope Fitzgerald's best novels. Fitzgerald was a writer who came to writing late: she published her first book, a biography of an English poet, at the age of fifty-eight, and she published her first novel two years later. Over the next twenty years or so—practically up to her death in 2000, at the age of eighty-three—she continued to develop as a novelist until she became an undisputed if rather strange master of the form. I'm thinking particularly about three of her late novels, each of which is set in a different place and time: *Innocence*, which occupies two Italys (the sixteenth-century incarnation that appears briefly at the beginning of the novel, and then the mid-twentieth-century version); *The Beginning of Spring*, which takes place in Russia in 1913; and *The Blue Flower*, which reproduces, or imagines, the atmosphere of Novalis's late-eighteenth-century Germany.

In all three books, the language Fitzgerald employs, while partaking of her usual qualities—authorial wit, refusal of closure, suppressed but tangible emotion—also contains something that is specific to its location. In *Innocence*, this has largely to do with rhythm, a kind of run-on, comma-separated pileup of clauses that somehow evokes the rapidity and vivacity of Italian speech. In *The Beginning of Spring*, it has more to do with tone: the conversations among the Anglo-Russian characters have both the philosophical intensity and the melancholy humor of late-nineteenth-century Russian prose, even as they also contain a note of British asperity. And in *The Blue Flower*, which is probably Fitzgerald's most extreme effort in this direction, the English is so heavily flavored as to seem, at times, a direct translation from the German. No, that's not quite right: not a translation, but an imagined German, the way German would sound in our minds if we knew it as fluently as we know English. It is English functioning as German while still retaining the flexibility of English.

This is especially clear in a phrase like "the Bernhard," which is how the family at the center of *The Blue Flower* (and, at times, the author) refer to the youngest son, a sprightly, original boy named Bernhard. Its sense in English is clear enough—a kind of family joke, a singling-out of the smallest, oddest child—and there are even English examples of a similar usage in children's nicknames: *The Piggle*, for instance, is a D. W. Winnicott case study about a little girl. But the phrase also evokes the German *der Bernhard*, which is a colloquial, sometimes regional way of expressing familiarity, as if to say, "Oh, that Bernhard! That is so typical of him." This is one of those authorial gifts we needn't fully receive to enjoy. That is, you can still get a kick out of the name "the Bernhard" even if you don't know the German habit of speech, but if you do know it, the phrase is made even richer.

The effect of such linguistic strategies (which go by much more quickly, and therefore with much more subtlety, than I have been able to suggest) is to create a sort of magically thin and nearly transparent scrim between us and the characters. We are looking directly at these people—inhabiting them, in some cases—but we are also looking at the medium through which they are brought to life. Fitzgerald's novels point to themselves as written objects and at the same time continue to insist on the psychological reality of their characters. They do not let us off the emotional hook in any way. On the contrary, they appear to strengthen our connection with the characters by making us feel that *all* of us, readers and characters alike, somehow recognize the existence of the transmitting paper and print. In *The Beginning of Spring*, this sense is reinforced by the fact that the main character, Frank Albertovich Reid, runs a Moscow-based printing business called Reidka's. There is always a special interest, I find, that attaches to novels focusing on the printing or paper business (Arnold Bennett's *Clayhanger* is one, and Balzac's *Lost Illusions* is another). In such novels, the object in your hands points, however indirectly, to the process of its own making, as if to level the difference between your reality and its own.

Yet that is not the only function of the linguistic scrim. It unites us with the characters, but it also sets us apart from them, as if to suggest with its veiling habit that all insights are partial and most questions unanswerable. When we reach the end of a Penelope Fitzgerald novel, we are generally at a loss. We do not know what will happen next; we may not even fully comprehend what has already happened. Like Henry James at the end of *The Bostonians*, but with much less of a melodramatic flourish, she leaves us in doubt. In keeping with this, her novels tend to hinge or even end on moments of spontaneous silence. It is in those wordless moments—the ones between the lines, or before the lines begin, or after they end—that her tales have their secret life. What she gives us on the page, she manages to suggest, is only a small part of what is really there.

If Penelope Fitzgerald is the mistress of this technique, then Joseph Conrad is its master. Very few of his novels or novellas come to a firm conclusion. Reaching the end of *Nostromo* or *Lord Jim*, the first-time reader almost invariably turns back to the beginning. One finishes *Heart of Darkness* and realizes that the warning in the title, though ill-heeded, meant what it said: clear answers will never be forthcoming. This obscurity may be in part a function of Conrad's deep-seated irony, an authorial distance from his characters so extreme that it lends an otherworldly despair to his work—as if God, say, had tried to see into mortal souls but then given it up as a bad job and abandoned us to our random fates. But there is something more human going on here as well, something that can be felt mainly at the level of language. Once again, there is that faint screen, that nearly indiscernible layer of mist, lying between us and the characters. It is not exactly a narrator (though in some of Conrad's works there is indeed a narrating figure superimposed on the story); it is more of a linguistic slippage. Perhaps this is due to the fact that his first language was Polish and his second French, so that English, when he came to it, always retained some of the tantalizing allure of the incompletely familiar. Perhaps it is due to something else entirely. Whatever the cause, Conrad's prose has a slightly alienated quality that makes it the perfect environment for inscrutable characters and their incomprehensible actions.

The two novels which seem to me to do this best—to present the inexplicable in a way that draws us completely inside and at the same time leaves us hanging—are *The Secret Agent* and *Under Western Eyes*. Both are political novels of a sort, and both reflect an anti-Russian bias that perhaps comes naturally to a Pole. But to be anti-Russian, in the sense of being suspicious of the tsarist government's autocratic and tentacular reach, is also to be very Russian indeed. It is precisely this attitude that Conrad shares with Turgenev, with Dostoyevsky, with Gogol, with Chekhov, and with all those other pre-revolutionary writers who would not necessarily have felt they had much in common with each other. This Russian atmosphere so permeates *Under Western Eyes* that the last time I read the novel, I found myself carelessly turning back to the title page to see who had done the translation. I caught myself and laughed, but my mistake had alerted me to a realization: that the novel's portrayal of Russian activists and Russian spies felt absolutely like a view from within, despite or perhaps even because of its terrifying Conradian irony.

Both the immersion and the distance are habits of mind he could have gleaned from the Russians, and no doubt did. For every writer that came after them, those towering nineteenth-century figures became the essential source, the standard to measure oneself against—and this is as true of writers from China and South Africa as it is for Europeans and Americans. No one had ever before learned to tell the truth as those great Russians did, and no one would ever do it better. I am not sure how to account for their superiority in this regard; I am not even sure how to describe it fully. But if I were to characterize what they had in common, one of the words I would use is authority.

FOUR

AUTHORITY

For those of us who came of age during a period of rebellion and unrest—whether in 1789, 1848, 1917, or 1968—the word is bound to carry a negative connotation. To some, it evokes uniforms, officialdom, governmental interference in the rights and activities of the private individual. To others, it suggests parents, teachers, clergymen, deans, and the whole range of unpleasant "authority figures" designed to prevent one from doing exactly as one wishes. In either case, it is seen as a bad thing, something to be dismantled or at the very least resisted.

But that is not at all the sense in which I mean it here. When I speak of authority in a work of literature, I am referring back to the word's root, its connection to the idea of authorship. The kind of authority one finds in a literary work is the opposite of the guns-and-uniforms kind (or even the spankings-and-homework kind). It has no legal power to enforce anything. It cannot punish or deprive. It depends for its effect on the acceptance, the acknowledgment, of those receiving it. The writer possesses authority, but only by virtue of the reader who senses it. Not everyone will discern authority in the same set of writers, and people will disagree about which elements give rise to it even if they agree it is there. It is one of the trickiest areas to discuss, and its presence in a given work is impossible to prove to anyone's complete satisfaction.

One reason it's always hard to point to literary authority is that it must be partially hidden to succeed. If the author speaks to us in too pushy a manner, or overwhelms his poor little characters with his own huge ego, or rests his hand too heavily on the wheel of the plot, we will fail to credit his creation as real—and real it must be to us, at least on some level, if we are to invest our time and emotions in it. The author who brings a literary work into being must make something out of nothing. He is like a magician in that respect, except he cannot take his bows or beg for our applause, because if we notice him whisking the rabbit out of the hat, we will realize the performance is an illusion.

And now, having written that sentence, I can immediately think of three or four exceptions to it: Shakespeare, through Prospero, begging for our applause at the end of *The Tempest*; Swift brandishing the rabbit *and* the hat at us in the footnotes to *A Tale of a Tub*; Cervantes examining quite explicitly the whole question of an author's authority; and all sorts of other examples from later in this chapter as well as earlier in this book. But I want to stress the way in which these exceptions prove the rule. They acknowledge the illusion precisely to get it out of the way, so that we can see that something else remains. They establish their own authority by being suspicious of authority in general, aligning themselves with our tendency to question authorial power and thus getting in ahead of us. What is left when they have done so—the residue, after our suspicions have been allayed—is what we take to be true.

The point of all this is that literature can never be *just* a trick. We need to feel that something more is at stake, that something is truly being created where nothing was before. So the author's involvement at a human level, his egotistical, self-serving, non-godlike manipulation of words and feelings, must be transformed in some way, disguised, made secret and powerful—though none of these words quite tell the story, because they imply deception, and the essence of authority is its truth.

Literary truths may have little or nothing to do with historical truth. The Furies and Satan are mythical figures brought to life by the power of their authors' imaginations, and the fact that many people once took them for actual beings has no effect, one way or the other, on how strongly I now credit them when I read the House of Atreus trilogy or *Paradise Lost*. Shakespeare borrowed his Cleopatra and his Richard II from history, but for me they are no more real than his Juliet and his Othello, whom he made up wholesale. Chaucer's Wife of Bath and Cervantes's Sancho Panza never existed or else existed in a thousand quotidian forms, but either way, each of them has a strongly marked individuality which transcends that of most individuals I have met. This is not to denigrate life, which must in some form be the source— if only a vaporous, indirect source—of all literary authority. It is simply to comment on the extent to which the made-up sometimes trumps the actual in terms of believability.

Authority, as I am using it, has nothing to do with the authoritarian. The work that commands us to believe in it by virtue of its right to govern our thoughts—*Pravda*, say, or *Mein Kampf*, or the more regulatory passages of Leviticus— will have little hold on our imaginations once that right has been removed. This is not just a matter of tone. It would be inaccurate to say that authoritarian works command while works with authority persuade, for even the word "persuasion"

is too blinkered, too end-achieving, too personally manipu-
lative to cover the methods employed by the most powerful
literature. (But the words "method," "employ," and "power"
are also suspect here. They are blunt instruments standing in
for something that is far more delicate and in fact nearly indiscernible.) The author who possesses authority has no palpable designs on us: we barely exist for him, just as he barely
exists for us. In the face of the literary work's reality, we
bystanders—the many readers, the sole writer—become non-
entities, like Shakespeare.

Which is not to say that we disappear entirely. The good
writer remains vitally present in every line he writes, and
even when the mortal author dies, the voice on the page is
still alive with that individuality. Nor can the reader ever
erase herself completely: there is no such thing as a purely
impersonal reading. We bring ourselves to everything we do,
and the more honestly and seriously we do it, the more we
bring along the whole of ourselves. So I would be lying if I
suggested that the two people engaged in the essential literary transaction, the writer and his reader, could ever vanish.
But their relation to each other becomes more, and less, than
personal. By virtue of the literary work over which they
meet, the reader and the writer both begin to loosen their
hold on selfhood. This is a grip that most of us maintain,
quite rightly, throughout our conscious lives; we need to do
so if we are not to be viewed as mad by ourselves and by others. I have nothing against selfhood. I rely on it daily, hourly
even, and it fuels a great deal of my existence. It even fuels
my existence as a reader, for that self is the one who chooses
to take up a given book, to finish it or put it down, to engage
with the characters, to see herself reflected in them. And yet
at some point in the process of reading, if the work has authority enough, the self yields. It ceases to have objections or

prejudices of its own. This is what allows the Buddhist to be gripped by *Paradise Lost*, the seasick-prone landlubber to immerse herself in *Moby-Dick*, the atheist to fall in love with *The Brothers Karamazov*.

Which brings us back to the Russian writers of the nineteenth and early twentieth centuries. These writers, it seems to me, are in possession of a uniquely powerful conviction, fully and effectively transmitted to us, that what they are putting down on the page, though it might be labeled "fiction," is the truth. More than any other comparable collection of writers, the Russians evidently believed that to tell the truth is literature's highest calling, its primary aim, superseding all the usual fripperies such as stylistic acrobatics, career advancement, obeisance to tradition, rebellion against tradition, and other common forms of authorial game-playing. This is not to say that they don't play games—they adore linguistic flourishes and newfangled constructions, as a quick glance at everything from Nikolai Gogol's surreal "The Nose" to Andrei Bely's fragmented, dreamlike *Petersburg* will suggest. But the games, however humorous, are always introduced for a serious purpose. They support the naked truth-telling even as they seem to embroider and disguise it.

There is, besides, our sense of the risks these writers have taken to bring us their truths. The risks needn't be bodily threats to survival (though they sometimes were), and they needn't be explicitly political or ideological (though some sort of politics was always a part of that Russian atmosphere, if only in the background). Yet something grave must be at stake. In order to imbue their words with the required weight, writers as different as Turgenev and Dostoyevsky, Gogol and Tolstoy, Goncharov and Herzen and Chekhov, must all convince us—quietly, almost invisibly, and without self-pity or self-aggrandizement—that it has cost them something to produce their revelations. The cost might be personal or public, psychological or economic, a nagging, constant loss or a violent, sudden one. Most likely it is a combination, and one that couldn't be defined or quantified even by the author himself. The point is that truth is not free or easily come by. And if it costs these writers something to reveal it, it also costs us something to take it in. That is why reading a novel like *Crime and Punishment* or *Fathers and Sons* can be so viscerally painful even as it also brings us a special kind of pleasure.

This is not to say that Russian literature is irreversibly solemn or grave. There can be humor (though, granted, always in a sharp, ironic vein), and there can even be extreme kindness. One of the most darkly humorous books of the period is Ivan Goncharov's *Oblomov*, which mingles a perspicacious eye for the truth with a strong sense of authorial generosity. If there is no hope for Ilya Ilyich Oblomov by the end, that is only a reflection of the character's own accurate self-assessment—and there does seem to be some version of hope available to others, if only of a tenuous, temporary kind.

I first tried reading *Oblomov* when I was in my twenties, but it bored me, for reasons that I now see reflected more on me than on the book. In my impatience, I could not last through the part of the novel (representing at least the first hundred pages or more) where Oblomov simply won't do anything. He won't submit himself to being dressed or shaved by his serf-servant; he won't allow his rooms to be cleaned; he won't handle his own urgent business matters; he won't read a novel, or visit friends, or go on pleasurable expeditions; in fact, he won't even get out of bed. When I was twenty-five, I figured I had got the picture (lazy Russian nobleman

in decline, representing whole lazy class in decline), and I
gave up.

But lately I picked it up and finished the entire book,
deciding in the course of my reading that this was one of the
great pieces of nineteenth-century literature, perhaps even
equal in quality to the works of Dostoyevsky and Turgenev,
but more akin in tone to, say, the Eça de Queirós of *The
Maias*. For what happens to Oblomov, in the parts of the novel
I had never made it through before, is that he falls in love
with a sensitive and intelligent young woman named Olga,
and she falls in love with him. Being Oblomov, he eventually
loses her through laziness, and then reverts to his previous
sloth; in this respect, we seem to be following the usual predetermined path of the tragic Russian figure. But the novel
does not end there. Olga goes on to marry Oblomov's friend
Andrei Stolz—a great character, and a great friend—and together Stolz and Olga try to rescue Oblomov from his life of
sleep. That they do not succeed does not necessarily mean the
novel ends unhappily, for though the title bears his name,
Oblomov is not the only character we care about here.

Imagine a version of *Remembrance of Things Past* in which
Marcel's lover Albertine, whom he is constantly doubting,
hiding, rejecting, and then wanting back, was able to fall in
love with someone else and end up happily with him (or her);
imagine a version that took us outside the mind of the everlasting Marcel and into the minds of other characters—
including not only Albertine, but also her new love, and not
only upper-class people, but also Marcel's housekeeper and
cook. Imagine a final volume in which we looked back on all
these people not just from the position of Marcel, as we do
in Proust's own *Past Recaptured*, but from the perspective of
a friend who outlives him. It would be a different book, of
course, and we would lose a great deal: Marcel's relentless

introversion is part of what makes him memorable as a narrator, and valuable to us. But something like this revised Proust
is what we get in *Oblomov*—a thoughtful, sharp-eyed, but
also generous look at particular characters in their particular
setting, with all the intelligence of a broad social commentary (for Oblomovism *was* a recognizable characteristic of
Russian aristocrats in decline: I was at least right about that,
in my callow youth), but with all the virtues of an astute
psychological novel as well. Goncharov's form of authorial
truth—a bit like Chekhov's, in this respect—mainly takes the
form of unanswerable questions voiced by the characters
themselves, whose lives the novel penetrates in a way that is
at once piercing and tender. I have never read anything else
quite like it, and certainly nobody had in 1858, when it first
came out in Russia.

Alexander Herzen, the great nonfiction writer and acti-
vist who died in exile in 1870, had some instructive ideas
about why the literature of his contemporaries carried the
authority it did. "The terrible consequences of human speech
in Russia necessarily give it added power," he wrote in his
masterpiece *My Past and Thoughts*, an autobiography which is
itself one of the key works of nineteenth-century Russian
literature. "The voice of a free man is welcomed with sympathy and reverence, because with us to lift it up one absolutely
must have something to say. One does not so lightly decide to
publish one's thoughts when at the end of every page one sees
looming a gendarme."

Herzen—who himself tried to write novels before set-
tling more comfortably into the nonfiction mode—attributes
Russia's literary achievements in large part to the national
and individual awareness of tragedy. Personal and collective
suffering, he suggests, are what account for the fictional
truth-telling. "The Russian novel is nothing but pathological

anatomy," he says; "it is only a statement of the evil that gnaws at us, a continual accusation of ourselves, without respite or pity." Contrasting his compatriots with Goethe and the other German idealists, he points out that in Russian literature "you do not hear a gentle voice come down from heaven, announcing to Faust forgiveness for sinful Gretchen. No consolation is sought: the only voices raised are those of doubt and damnation." Yet it is this very descent into negativity—a mode Herzen characterizes as "Melancholy, skepticism, irony . . . the three chief strings of the Russian lyre"—that offers the only real hope for redemption. "He who frankly avows his defects feels that there is something in him that can escape and resist his downfall; he understands that he can redeem his past," Herzen concludes.

In his own calmly secular way (and Herzen is truly our contemporary in this regard, as in so many others), he was able to put into such words both Dostoyevsky's view and Chekhov's, both the self-lacerating despair of the deeply religious man and the darkly humorous, skeptical vision of the scientific humanist. They are very different kinds of authority, it would seem, but in the remarkably unified world of Russian literature, they speak with a similar urgency and a similar strength. And they speak to us still. That is perhaps the oddest thing of all: that we needn't come from Russia, or live under the tsars, or believe in the orthodoxies or counter-orthodoxies of that time and place (or even know what they were, in any great detail), to understand that what is being conveyed to us is the truth. Whether it will be true for all time is impossible for me to say, but I cannot imagine a world in which Oblomov and Rasknolnikov, Prince Andrei and Uncle Vanya, would not have a recognizable reality. I would not want to live in such a world, for it would have ceased in some essential way to be human.

This is probably not something I need to worry about. The slight, the facile, and the merely self-glorifying tend to drop away over the centuries, and what we are left with is the bedrock: Homer and Milton, the Greek tragedians and Shakespeare, Chaucer and Cervantes and Swift, Dostoyevsky and Tolstoy and James and Conrad. Time does not make their voices fainter. On the contrary, it reinforces our sense of their truth-telling capacity.

Literary authority is not something that appears only in life-or-death circumstances. The nineteenth-century Russians may have been its masters because of their unusual situation in history, but each era, however debased, has its own version of it. In my daily life as an editor, I encounter it mainly in fleeting form, in the first sentences of a very small percentage of the submissions that arrive at *The Threepenny Review*. Such a sentence is like a beacon seen from afar, an instantly recognizable source of hope. This kind of authority can come from anyone—a young, unpublished writer, a seasoned professional, a hidden genius working alone, a long-dead master revisited in translation. It is not entirely a matter of voice, though voice enters into it. It is rarely a matter of subject, though certain topics signal its likely absence. A story that begins "When I was in second grade," for instance, almost never possesses a sense of authority. Nor do stories that start with Mom and Dad fighting, or an older sister being mean, or a boyfriend or girlfriend insisting on a breakup. This is not because such events are untrue to life. On the contrary, everyone has been through them. You might say that they are *too* true to life. The material has not yet been sifted by the imagination, recast in a way that turns it into literature. It remains in the realm of what anyone, with or without literary ability, might think or say.

There is nothing wrong with the quotidian. We all, or almost all, dwell in that realm. But to have authority, a literary work must be able to turn the quotidian into something strange—as, for instance, Beckett does in his plays, or Kafka in his stories. These writers obviously have an uncanny aspect, an affinity for the patently unreal, but it is in fact their obsession with routine life, over and above the strangeness that punctuates it, which distinguishes these masters from their less eerie, more wilfully bizarre imitators. One can't just try for strangeness, as it turns out: a too-obvious effort to surprise is just as bad as straight dullness. Stories that start "I never thought I would see a zombie in Macy's" or "Paul, waving a loaded gun in my face, told me to shut up" get put into the rejection pile as quickly as those about second grade or a mean older sister. The latter kind of story presumes that everything about the writer's daily life will interest us; the former assumes that nothing will, and that therefore the writer needs to lie or fantasize to get our attention. Kafka never lies, and neither does Beckett. Even their wildest exaggerations—a boy turning into a bug, old people housed in garbage cans—smack of a felt truth.

It is easier to disguise lack of authority in a third-person story than in a first-person one. Somehow the distance imposed simply by the pronoun "he" or "she" allows the writer greater room to maneuver, making the narrator seem more knowledgeable or at least more coolly reflective than the naked, breast-beating "I." But this too is a deception, and it will wear off within a couple of sentences if the literary work is no good. Fake situations and fake emotions are surprisingly easy to spot in fiction. The literary work, however far-fetched, has to ring true for the fiction to carry the weight of our potential suspicion. (If we are not suspicious at all, it is because we have given up, as readers, and are just killing time. That is what "trash reading" means.) This credibility is not just a matter of the author believing what she is saying. We too must on some level believe it, even if we know it to be made up. Especially when we know it to be made up.

Authority, though, is not the same as the absence of doubt. I would go so far as to suggest that all the most convincing works of literature must possess an element of doubt. That is the calling card with which they delicately persuade us to open our doors to them; it is the proof that they do not intend to deceive us. And if this is true at the beginning of a novel, a story, or a poem, it is even more noticeably true at the end. A question will always hover over the authoritative author's conclusions, so that they are not merely conclusions, but also an opening out, a releasing of other possibilities. Occasionally the openness can take the form of an actual question, as in Kay Ryan's "How can something / so grand and serene / vanish again and again / without a hint?"—the last line of her brief poem "Tune," which itself comes at the end of her collection *The Best of It*. But much more often it will appear in the form of an assertion that contains and nourishes its own self-contradiction.

Henry James specialized in such conclusions, and the effect is to make us wonder all over again, every time we read the novel, how it is going to turn out, even if we already know. "We shall never be again as we were," says one of the two protagonists at the end of *The Wings of the Dove*. Yes, but which of the two lovers says it, Merton Densher or Kate Croy? I challenge you to guess from memory, and then check yourself. I think you are more likely than not to be wrong, as I was the last time I read the book. It is like the end of *The Brothers Karamazov*, where you can't remember from one reading to the next whether Dmitri is guilty or not. He is both guilty and not guilty, just as Kate and Merton are equally capable of saying that line (or of thinking it, before the other

has said it). A novel like James's or Dostoyevsky's has authority partly because it turns out to be larger—in its scope, in its
outcomes—than anything the author could have planned. He
brings his novel to an ending because he has to, but in some
ways it also keeps going without him. The conclusion must
be credible enough to satisfy, but part of its credibility is that
it can never *fully* satisfy.

Of course, all these laws exist to be violated. (That too is
one sign of authority, the writer's willingness and ability to
break the rules.) Wendell Berry can write a story about when
he was in second grade and make it work. I hadn't remembered it this way, but when I went back to look at one of his
autobiographical Andy Catlett stories, I found that his first
line was actually quite close to the opening I have been de-
ploring: "In grades one and two I was a sweet, tractable child
who caused no trouble." Yet I think that even here, in just
these few words, you can sense the imposition of a certain
distance, something that makes this other than a bald, flat
presentation of childhood experience. Listen to how another
of these Catlett stories starts: "Early in my childhood, when
the adult world and sometimes my own experience easily
assumed the bright timelessness of myth, I overheard my father's friend Charlie Hardy telling about the drouth of 1908."
Or still another, which begins: "Andy Catlett was a child of
two worlds." The voice is the same, whether it is inside or
outside the main character. It is a voice that simultaneously
lives through events and recalls them, experiencing the child's
emotions and perceptions even as it reflects on them from a
position of age. A young person could not write these stories;
Wendell Berry himself couldn't have written them when he
was young.

But the fact that Berry's authority comes from age—the
fact that he has actually managed to learn something in the

course of his many decades, and not just pass through them—
does not mean that all authority needs to come from the elderly. In the same issue of *The Threepenny Review* that ran one
of those Andy Catlett stories was another piece of fiction by a
young, barely published writer named Shashi Bhat. "Aarthi
kept her receipts punctured through their middles on a bent
coat hanger, which she placed in a corner to avoid injury"
begins this story about a helpless, hapless miser in her mid-
twenties. The narrative voice does not pretend to a larger view
than that of its named character, and yet there is a breadth, a
strength here that goes beyond the merely anecdotal. One can
locate it partly in the absence of ostentation (the sentence has
no adverbs whatsoever, and only a single, necessary adjec-
tive), as well as in the subtle, distant humor of that "to avoid
injury." You would have to read the whole story to be sure, but
if you came upon just this one sentence in a stack of undif-
ferentiated manuscripts, it would beam at you like a lighthouse
at sea.

Is this kind of authority the same as literal truth? No. I do
not have to believe that Shashi Bhat has lived a miser's life to
appreciate her story. I can suspect—indeed, I can know—that
Andy Catlett shares many qualities and experiences with his
author, but this knowledge is finally irrelevant to my evalua-
tion of Wendell Berry's fiction. The story works convinc-
ingly on the page or it does not work at all, and whatever
knowledge the author possesses must be subsumed into the
fiction for it to come across as believable fact. Tolstoy, they
say, disregarded actual military records and set forth a number of false or imagined details in his depictions of Napole-
onic battles. This does nothing to dampen our collective and
justified sense of belief in the authority of *War and Peace*. Its
truths exist at a deeper level than that of normal reportage or
demonstrable history. They echo our experience of the world,

and at the same time they teach us things we didn't know about the world before we encountered them in Tolstoy's pages.

This equilibrium is a delicate one, and it is always shifting, for we do not read literature from a fixed position. We change as we read, and not only because of what we read. I, for instance, read *War and Peace* for the first time mainly to find out whom Natasha would marry. At the age of twenty-two, I cared excessively about young women and their marriage possibilities, perhaps, in part, because I myself was a young woman who had no likely marriage in sight. So the Peace parts were the only sections of the book that really held my interest; I flipped through the War parts as if they were so many obstacles in my way. It was only when I came back to the novel some thirty years later that I understood how much I had missed. I had been looking for another *Anna Karenina*, in my youth, but *War and Peace* now strikes me as a much greater book, and it is the War sections that make it so.

If authority of the kind I am speaking about here—not historical authority, not legal authority, not even moral authority, exactly, though it may have something to do with that—is not completely identifiable with everyday truth-telling, then even less is it congruent with what we might call authenticity. There is nothing "authentic" (except in the sense of being old and original) about Homer's *Odyssey* or Shakespeare's *Tempest*, and in quite a different way there is nothing authentic about Beckett's *Endgame* or Kafka's *Castle*. No one could point to the experiences recounted there and say, "Yes, I've seen exactly this, I've done exactly that." These works bear only the most tangential relationship to reality as we know it. That the relationship is nonetheless important, indeed essential, does not mitigate the degree of its tangentiality. Literature is made up. (And this is true even of nonfiction literature, where the "I" is the author's careful construct and the rest has been heavily edited.) As Plato said, all poets are liars. This does not mean we should mistrust them. Only lies—lies of a particular type, lies that are the creations of great authors—have the capacity to convey certain kinds of truths to us.

Literature is, among other things, an undermining of the coherent worldview. Things can only be true in a specific way, for one reader at a time, at a particular moment in that reader's life. This may not seem like much, but it turns out to be a great deal, because it happens over and over, each time in a different way. The truths in literature are incidental and cumulative, not global and permanent. In some moods I think that those are the only kinds of truths that really matter.

A writer who clearly stands with me on this is D. H. Lawrence. Or perhaps it would be more accurate to say that I stand with him. Literature may be made up, but it is also borrowed, even stolen (as that line is itself borrowed from T. S. Eliot, who remarked in one of his essays that immature poets imitate, mature poets steal). I am constantly surprised by how much of my own mind is composed of the ideas of others, and so it is in this case. A few days after writing the preceding paragraphs, I ran across this passage from D. H. Lawrence's *Studies in Classic American Literature*: "Art-speech is the only truth. An artist is usually a damned liar, but his art, if it be art, will tell you the truth of his day. And that is all that matters. Away with eternal truth. Truth lives from day to day, and the marvellous Plato of yesterday is chiefly bosh today." I cite this not as any kind of scholarly authority (Lawrence would be horrified to think he could ever be called as *that* kind of witness), but because I find his sentences beautifully persuasive, and it gives me immense pleasure to write them down.

As it happens, this brief paragraph of Lawrence's appears on the same page as the lines I most often quote from him: "Never trust the artist. Trust the tale." These may not be the most powerful or touching words D. H. Lawrence ever wrote, but they are certainly the most useful. I recite them in almost every class I teach—to keep students from jumping to conclusions inspired by biographical or historical knowledge, to defeat the assaults of gender-based or other theory-inspired criticism, to rein in any tendencies toward know-it-all assertion, and, above all, to undermine the supposed authority of the artist's own statements about what he was setting out to do. The effect, as Lawrence no doubt intended, is to remove any possibility of proof. The writer's own spoken words about his mission and its accomplishment might be taken as evidence, legalistically, if we were to allow the artist to speak. But the tale makes no direct statements (if, indeed, it makes any statements at all). It can only be interpreted, and that job is finally up to each of us individually. We can get help from our predecessors, and we can rely to a certain extent on collective agreement, but in the end the decision to trust must be our own. To attribute the only authority to the tale itself is to foil any direct access we might have to an authoritative view.

And yet Lawrence was by no means giving away the whole store. As you can tell from his tone, he very much relied on his own version of authority. He was emphatic almost to the point of hysteria. He was convinced that when he wrote, he was writing the truth—and this conviction applied at least as much to matters of opinion and fiction as it did to fact. (Actually, it applied nearly exclusively to those more debatable areas: in the few cases where Lawrence wrote about factual matters, such as the look of the Sardinian landscape, his tone was much less aggressive.) Ranting and railing are

Lawrence's default mode, and this is true equally of the essays and the fictional works—though it is somewhat less true of the stories, and rarely true of the poems, which is why some people who can't bear the novels can still appreciate his poetry.

A lot of people can't bear the novels, and this has been true since they first began appearing in the early twentieth century. Time has not dulled their capacity to irritate. I still can't stomach *Lady Chatterley's Lover*, and *The Plumed Serpent* sends me into a rage, when it does not send me into fits of disbelieving giggles. But I know of no book more true than *Sons and Lovers*. I would stake my life on its truths about mothers and their sons, young women and their lovers; I *have* staked my life on them, at key moments of emotional crisis or existential despair.

There are many opinions floating around in *Sons and Lovers*, and only some of them belong to the author. The characters have very strong views about their lives, and about their desire to interfere with other lives, and about their desperation to get away from such interference, whether instigated by themselves or others. These people are bundles of conflicting emotions, with the conflicts running both between and within individuals. The sight of them trying to disentangle themselves reminds one of those demonic hand toys that capture your fingers and won't let them go, so that the harder you try to pull away, the more tightly you are gripped. The feelings in *Sons and Lovers* are alive, and they are alive *now*; they reignite every time you or I or anyone else reads the book.

You might be tempted to say, well, yes, that's what happens when an author knows enough to leave his characters alone and lets them develop into credible people, unintruded on by his manipulations, wishes, and commands. But the thing is, Lawrence *doesn't* leave his characters alone. He persecutes them, harasses them, invades them. He is forever chivvying them along and nipping at their heels. His animus against Walter Morel (the poor dumb brute of a miner who sires the novel's main character, the blatantly autobiographical Paul Morel) is so powerful that we end up resisting it. If Lawrence is going to gang up against his own character in this way, we feel morally obliged to take that character's side. Was Lawrence completely out of control here? Did he hate his own father so much he just couldn't help himself? But wait—never trust the artist, trust the tale. David Herbert Lawrence the person may have had it in for his father, but the novel *Sons and Lovers* knows enough to allow for our sympathy for Walter Morel. The book wouldn't work without it. So even as the author is ostensibly browbeating us with his opinions, he is also giving us the freedom to choose, to believe him or not, to side with whichever character we feel like siding with. That is the true sign of the writer's authority.

I have been making so many broad assertions that my readers may well feel their credulity exhausted. So perhaps now would be a good time to introduce a few specific illustrations, a few examples of how authority seems to me to exist in particular passages.

A writer's own special kind of authority may pervade every sentence in her work, but it is often most noticeable at the very beginning, where we are deciding whether or not to trust that voice, whether or not to enter that world into which we are being invited. If one were to compile a list of persuasive openings, one might start with *Pride and Prejudice*'s "It is a truth universally acknowledged, that a single man in

possession of a fortune must be in want of a wife." But that
would be unfair. Jane Austen is beyond competition: she carries so much authority in her quietly confident voice that she
can afford to mock even the idea of authority, at least as it
might be manifested in "universally acknowledged" truths.
So if we want to compare different levels of authority, we'd
do best to leave her out of it, just as for the moment we'll
leave out all the rest of the nineteenth-century novelists—for
their strength has already been tested by time, and it will be
hard to find any who do *not* seem to write with more authority than our contemporaries.

Let us look instead at a twentieth-century opening that is
almost as self-confident as Jane Austen's, though in place of
her apparent straightforwardness and simplicity, it substitutes
convolution and opacity. This is not an objection in itself.
Many wonderful novelists—Dickens, Melville, Henry James,
Marcel Proust, to list just the obvious—can write sentences
that go on for half a page, unfurling their clauses and delay-
ing their central points in a positively Germanic fashion.
Complexity is not at all the same thing as artificiality or self-
promotion, and simplicity of structure or language is not the
only form of authority. Here, then, is the opening sentence of
William Faulkner's *Absalom, Absalom!*:

> From a little after two o'clock until almost sundown of the
> long still hot weary dead September afternoon they sat in
> what Miss Coldfield still called the office because her father
> had called it that—a dim hot airless room with the blinds all
> closed and fastened for forty-three summers because when
> she was a girl someone had believed that light and moving
> air carried heat and that dark was always cooler, and which
> (as the sun shone fuller and fuller on that side of the house)
> became latticed with yellow slashes full of dust motes which
> Quentin thought of as being flecks of the dead old dried

paint itself blown inward from the scaling blinds as wind might have blown them.

Faulkner's prose leaves us breathless—literally so, in the way it forces us to exhale when its largely unpunctuated length is read out loud, and metaphorically too, in the degree to which it impresses without trying to. This single sentence invites us inside a particular place and time, introduces us to a couple of characters, and hints at their history, all the while using language that, if they could write, might have come from the characters themselves. The novel it introduces will clearly be requiring a great deal of us. This confiding, challenging voice presumes that, among other things, we will be able to focus our attention on small visual details, keep track of the complex strands of intertwined stories, recognize the undying effects of the past, both distant and recent, on the present, and appreciate the sound of a nearly musical language. We are deep into Faulkner territory here, that strange place which is an amalgam of external and internal, a community of unspoken thoughts and hidden reservations, a shared history that also belongs to each person alone. No one else has ever written quite like this, but one doesn't sense that this is because Faulkner is *trying* to be different. The language just reflects the way his mind works; he is simply (though it is a simplicity filled with difficulty and extenuation) putting down what he sees, what he imagines. The wisdom, if there is wisdom here—and I think there is a great deal—is lightly worn. Its pertinence to the wider world, to *our* world, is disguised as the minute observation of a particular society that Faulkner knew as well as Jane Austen knew hers.

A novel's opening lines don't have to be specific, and they don't have to be concrete—though if they are, the author will have an easier time winning us over. But an author who is willing to take risks can get away with almost anything, if he has enough intelligence and uses it with serious moral intent. Take this opening of a relatively recent J. M. Coetzee novel, *Elizabeth Costello*, whose first chapter is titled "Realism": "There is first of all the problem of the opening, namely, how to get us from where we are, which is, as yet, nowhere, to the far bank. It is a simple bridging problem, a problem of knocking together a bridge. People solve such problems every day. They solve them, and having solved them push on." This is a bit like Chaucer's "Go, litel bok," or Shakespeare's imagined actor "boying" Cleopatra in the posture of a whore. Bravely, recklessly, Coetzee is reminding us at the very beginning of his fiction that he is just making everything up, creating a world out of nothing, getting us from our "there" to his "here." But the fiction in which he does this is a novel about a fiction writer named Elizabeth Costello, so the problem outlined in these initial sentences—the problem of how to bridge the gap from our world to the realistic novel's world, and make that bridge sustain the weight of our potential disbelief—is both his problem and his main character's. Are these opening sentences his views, or hers? We are not required to choose.

Right from the start, the authority of the author is being questioned, just as it was in Austen's opening sally. And yet the effect in Coetzee is one of grave seriousness rather than, or perhaps in addition to, wit. That the seriousness will not weigh us down is signaled by the conversational tone of the abstract discussion: the short, direct clauses and sentences, the reliance on what sounds like common sense ("People solve such problems every day"). Both Coetzee and his Costello are aware that the solutions are not easy, if you are a novelist. They both feel the threat of failure. But they are repeatedly willing to try. And part of what enables them to keep on trying is the sense that other people in their line of work have faced—and solved, and then had to solve all over again, every time anew—the problem of how to get started.

There is no progress in the world of letters, as there is, say, in science or manufacturing. As the centuries pass, we do not get better or smarter at reading, and the authors among us do not get better at writing. Things come and go, make sense to us or not, depending on our particular state of mind, and we change our minds over the course of a lifetime. The whole culture can change its mind, too, but this doesn't necessarily mean that a work of literature gets dated forever. On the contrary, a book from 1814 can make sense to someone in 2014 in a way that it did not, perhaps, make sense to that person's great-grandmother in 1914. It is all a matter of what we believe, what we feel, coming into contact with the convictions and emotions expressed in the novel or poem or play.

In this respect—in its lack of progress—literature is similar to human life, individually and in the aggregate. In my own reading experience, I've found no one who recognized this more clearly than Alexander Herzen. What is encouraging about him is that he was able to hold in his mind two seemingly conflicting ideas: that there is no destined progress in our lives, and that it is nonetheless worth struggling for principles we believe in (such as the innate value of an individual life, or the need for equality and justice, or the importance of art). Here's how he put it in *My Past and Thoughts*, in a section where he was criticizing "the idol of *progress*" and its proponents:

Is it not simpler to grasp that man lives not for the *fulfilment of his destiny*, not for the incarnation of an idea, not for progress, but solely because he was born; and he was born *for* (however bad a word that is) . . . for the present, which does not at all prevent his either receiving a heritage from the past or leaving something in his will. To idealists this seems humiliating and coarse: they will take absolutely no account of the fact that the great significance of us men [. . .] consists in just this: that while we are alive, until the knot held together by us has been resolved into its elements, *we are for all that ourselves*, and not dolls destined to suffer progress.

And the same is true, it seems to me, of works of literature. They exist in and for themselves, without a purpose, without a destiny, without any intent to build upon each other into something larger. This does not mean that they have no connection to their ancestors and descendants— they do, just as we do, and the web of history holds them all together just as it holds us (at least in retrospect, which is how we generally view history). We can be individuals and still exist in relation to the collective life of our kind, just as books can. For us to be firmly lodged in the present, our own present, doesn't mean we have no awareness of the past or the future. It's just that this train of events is not necessarily going anywhere.

There is something liberating in this notion, once you get over the frightening sense of being untethered from certainty and destination. If you resolve to meet each work of literature one-to-one, reaching across from your own perspective to *its* own perspective, you will find that certain problems, certain dilemmas, simply drop away. There is no question of the present's superiority to the past, but nor is there any issue of the past's superiority to us. We are all equals, meeting as if on level ground. If anyone is able to brandish superior knowledge at the other, it is by virtue of having gained it in her own lifetime, in her own way—not because she happens to come from a more knowledgeable time. The knowledge, in any case, is only useful to the extent it is capable of being transmitted, so the reader, as receiver, becomes as important in this transaction as the author who transmits.

We can have many chances to receive: it is not all or nothing with books, as it is with a live performance or an actual event in history. You can go back to the book at different times in your life (as I went back to *War and Peace*) and receive what it has to offer you at that point, which may be neither more nor less in quantity than what you received before, but will almost certainly be different in kind. This is not progress; it may not even be accumulation, since your earlier impression may be replaced by a later one; but it will nonetheless be a kind of truth. "Truth lives from day to day," as Lawrence said, and the one you grasp on the fly is the only one there is, as far as literature goes—as far as any art goes. Such truths will not be susceptible to proof, but if there is to be no progress, and if each encounter with a literary work matters purely for its own sake, then the absence of proof doesn't really matter. The work speaks to you or it does not. That is all you can finally say.

In the English language, over the past four or five centuries, nobody has spoken to more of us—nobody has, in this sense, possessed more of what I am calling authority—than Shakespeare. He has been vilified by English schoolboys and eminent Russian novelists; he has been bowdlerized and travestied by Victorian theater producers, who sought to replace his tragic endings with more commercially viable happy ones; he has been abused by the Germans (who felt that Schlegel's translations of Shakespeare were far superior to the originals) and disdained by the French (who found him messy and verbose in comparison to his contemporary, Racine). He has been borrowed by each succeeding ideology to prove that its own perspective is the only correct one, and his work has lent itself to social commentary of all stripes, including the apolitical, purely psychological stripe. And yet he endures, always and only himself, available as freshly as ever to each new generation of readers and viewers.

We know so little about Shakespeare the man that the Lawrentian problem hardly exists in his case. There *is* no artist, just the tale. But what tale is it? Which performance, when they are all so different, is the definitive one? Can there be a final, perfect version of a Shakespeare play on the stage—and if not, does the literary work only exist in a kind of ghostly form, waiting to be tentatively, imperfectly embodied by each new approach?

I have opinions about these matters, but I do not have the answers. No one does. This is why Shakespeare raises to such an intense degree the question of authority. There are no operating instructions handed down to us by the writer (as there were, say, with T. S. Eliot's "The Waste Land" and James Joyce's *Ulysses*), and there are no regulations issued by the estate (as there notoriously have been in Beckett's case). In terms of productions, anything goes. You can put a piece of toast on the stage and call it *The Merchant of Venice*, and no one can stop you. We want to be able to say that the piece of toast is not Shakespeare—we know this, even if we cannot prove it. But how far does this knowledge go? Is a *Merchant of Venice* in modern dress Shakespeare? Is a *Merchant of Venice* done in blackface or by an all-female cast Shakespeare? Is a *Merchant of Venice* performed in German and set in a Mercedes Benz factory Shakespeare? (I have actually seen that version, done by the Berliner Ensemble, and it was one of the high points in a lifetime of theater-going.) Different people will get off this coach at different stages, and there is no firm point at which we will all be able to say in unison: *Now* it has passed beyond the pale. Now it is toast, not Shakespeare.

There is still another bothersome question about Shakespeare's authority, and that is, how do we hear it? In a play—which by definition has no narrator, and in which the only words are the characters' lines—there are no sentences we can point to as stemming specifically from the author. (It would be silly in any play to insist that the author's presence is felt only in the stage directions, and in Shakespeare's case it is not even an issue, because he used almost no stage directions.) Yet those of us who love Shakespeare love him, in particular, for his authority. He creates a world for us, and that world feels incomparably right, and true. He does not seem capable of setting a foot wrong, not at the line level, where the poetry is perhaps the best ever written, and not at the structural level, where everything coheres into a profound theatrical experience. If there are problems in the plays—the anti-Semitism in *The Merchant of Venice*, the stern, cruel justice in *Measure for Measure*—these are *our* problems, the result of our not yet having figured out how to cope with the disturbing material. Plays that once seemed equally intractable, such as *Othello*, *The Tempest*, and *The Winter's Tale*, have turned out to be audience favorites, now that the sticky patches have been resolved—resolved, I mean, in a way that leaves the underlying darkness and conflict intact. Such problems can only be solved temporarily, for each new generation raises new sensitivities, new concerns. That too is a source of Shakespeare's continuing authority: his infinite flexibility, his adaptability to the needs and sensibilities of each era.

All this makes him seem like a miracle worker, or even a god. And I do believe, in my thoroughly agnostic way, that

Shakespeare's plays are small miracles. Like the ancient Greek temples left standing on the southern shores of Italy, they seem not to stem from powers we think of as human. And yet they *are* human; and unlike the ruined temples, Shakespeare's plays even feel human in scale. Side by side with the hugeness and the impressiveness of his work is something much smaller, much more graspable, much more easily recognized. If Shakespeare at times comes across as a grand remnant of the oversized past—one of those monumental "bare ruin'd choirs," to quote his own line—he is also our most intimate mirror, the one in the bathroom perhaps, where we casually catch our own faces morning and night, hardly even aware of what we are seeing.

FIVE

GRANDEUR AND INTIMACY

Consider the emotion we call love. Which category would you put it in? Is it a grand, consuming passion, bigger than anything else we experience on earth? Or is it the very essence of intimacy, the closest we ever approach to another human being? For Shakespeare, it can be both.

Look, for example, at what he does with *Antony and Cleopatra*. In this complicated drama—at once a love story, a history play, and a tragedy—he gives us two larger-than-life figures whose passion for each other ultimately brings about their deaths. Everything we hear about Cleopatra—from the famous description of her by Antony's friend Enobarbus ("Age cannot wither her, nor custom stale / Her infinite variety") to the manner in which Antony himself addresses her (he often calls her "Egypt," as if to equate her with her whole country)—suggests her outsized personality, her enormous power. Her strength is evident even in retreat, as Antony discovers when he finds himself following her after she flees during a sea battle against Caesar. "O, my lord, my lord, / Forgive my fearful sails! I little thought / You would have followed," she cries, to which he responds:

> Egypt, thou knew'st too well
> My heart was to thy rudder tied by th' strings,
> and thou shouldst tow me after. O'er my spirit
> Thy full supremacy thou knew'st, and that
> Thy beck might from the bidding of the gods
> Command me.

For a man like Antony, this is what it means to be in love: you cede to someone else a control over you that is even greater than your own sense of honor. It is a painful position for him to find himself in, and it is to his credit, as a lover, that he only rarely allows this awareness to interfere with his passion for Cleopatra. Or perhaps it is precisely the nature of his passion that it *can't* be interfered with, even if the enslavement sometimes chafes. (We can hear it chafing in that repetition of the slightly accusing "thou knew'st.")

But to Cleopatra it is Antony who is the greater force, the immortal figure. After his death, and shortly before her own, she reflects longingly:

> I dreamt there was an Emperor Antony . . .
> His legs bestrid the ocean, his reared arm
> Crested the world: his voice was propertied
> As all the tunèd spheres . . .
> Think you there was or might be such a man
> As this I dreamt of?

The question is seriously meant—this is, among other things, Shakespeare asking us whether any mortal person could be as huge as the Antony created by his and Cleopatra's fertile imaginations—but it is also the kind of self-mocking, painful, slightly flirtatious joke that Cleopatra is in the habit of making. For the man she addresses with this question is an emissary of Caesar's; and when the Roman answers, "Gentle

madam, no" (it was, after all, a dream, so what else is he supposed to say?), she lashes out at him, "You lie, up to the hearing of the gods." The gods are frequently invoked by these
two lovers when they speak about each other, as if they both
consider their love affair to be so gigantic as to be noticeable
even from a heavenly distance. And the phrase conjures up a
theatrical distance as well: in Shakespeare's time, as now, the
cheap, high seats in English theaters were known as "the gods,"
so this line of Cleopatra's, like that other one about an actor
boying her greatness, once again places her both inside and
outside the play, in her time and also in ours.

The grandeur, then, is evident. But what about the
intimacy? Fleeting examples of it are scattered throughout
the play—in Enobarbus's odd description of how he saw
Cleopatra "hop forty paces through the public street," in
Eros's tender words just before he kills himself to avoid killing Antony—but I will focus here on a single scene, where
Antony and Cleopatra have been arguing about the fact that
she let one of Caesar's emissaries kiss her hand. Antony is in
such a jealous fury that he becomes downright insulting:
"Have I my pillow left unpressed in Rome / Forborne the
getting of a lawful race, / And by a gem of women, to be
abused / By one that looks on feeders?" She tries to interject
a soothing word or two, but he continues to berate her for
minutes on end, even as he has Caesar's man soundly whipped.
Finally he sneers, "To flatter Caesar, would you mingle eyes /
With one that ties his points?"

"Not know me yet?" she responds, invoking all their
shared history in a few words.

And this, though he has been in a towering rage, appears
to catch him up. "Cold-hearted toward me?" he asks in what
seems a rather sudden turnabout. I suppose that line *could* be
delivered in a taunting or sarcastic tone, but it makes more

sense if the actor says it with an almost apologetic tenderness, as if inviting her to join him in ending their spat. She, at any rate, accepts that invitation: "Ah, dear, if I be so, / From my cold heart let heaven engender hail, / And poison it in the source, and the first stone / Drop in my neck . . ."—and there we are, back in the grand manner, with the gods overseeing the behavior of the oversized lovers. But that "ah, dear" has another tone entirely, a nearly domestic tone. And so does another line of hers that comes only a few seconds later, after they have kissed and made up. "It is my birthday," Cleopatra announces out of the blue. "I had thought t'have held it poor. But since my lord / Is Antony again, I will be Cleopatra." I have always wondered if it really *was* her birthday, or if she just made that up on the spur of the moment, to give them something extra to celebrate. In any case, the idea of a privately remembered birthday (as opposed to the massive, preplanned public occasion one would normally associate with a monarch of Cleopatra's stature) makes her seem winningly personal. It is part of her infinite variety, no doubt, that she can sometimes seem as tiny and mortal as we are.

You can find passages like this in Shakespeare's other great tragedies—in *King Lear*, for instance, in the scenes between Lear and Edgar, where the real madman treats the fake madman with unusual kindness; or in *Macbeth*, when Macduff has trouble taking in the news that his family has been slaughtered, and so keeps repeating himself in disbelief. In each case, what makes the intimate moment so noticeable is the grandeur of the surrounding play. The characters, speaking in poetry that in no way resembles ordinary speech, have been presented to us as something hugely admirable or terrible (or, generally, both), something beyond the merely human. So when they descend to a moment of ordinariness, the pathos is extraordinary. It is the sudden change of scale that does it.

The balance will vary, of course. Some works (the plays of Aeschylus and Sophocles, Milton's *Paradise Lost*, Conrad's *Nostromo*, Melville's *Moby-Dick*) seem to lean heavily toward the grand. Others (the novels of Henry James, Edith Wharton, Jane Austen) come across as mainly intimate—though even as I say that, I can think of ways in which that's not really true: James certainly has his moments of grandeur, especially in the language, and Wharton's *Custom of the Country*, though it's a very good novel, strikes me as neither intimate nor grand. They are slippery categories, these two. It's possible, I suppose, to see everything as falling somewhere on the spectrum between them, if one tries hard enough. But I'm more interested, for the moment, in looking at what a literary work is doing when it brings together these two things that seem like opposites (though, granted, they may turn out not to be opposites).

Grandeur does not imply grandiosity. When it appears in literature, its claim to largeness has been well earned; it is not the result of delusional narcissism or boastful hype. It may partake of what we think of as "the grand manner," but it is not annoying in the way people who assume the grand manner often are. Literary grandeur is not snobbish. Rather than alienating or diminishing us, it enlarges us with its own largeness, and we find ourselves readily assenting to its outsized views. Those views tend to be panoramic or telescopic in nature (though not exclusively so), and they lend us a perspective that is often lacking in our regular life. This can be achieved with high-flown vocabulary and complicated syntax, but it can be done equally well through a cool austerity, a shriven bareness. Beckett's plays, in their own down-in-the-dumps way, are no less grand than those of Sophocles, for both authors aim to get at some kind of massive truth that is hidden behind the facades of daily existence. That this truth is something dark and frightening, though also cathartic and in that sense exhilarating, is partly what gives these works their stirring intensity.

That feeling of being stirred is one of the ways you can recognize grandeur in a work of art. It's possible to be briefly stirred by false grandeur, and you need to be on your guard against deceptions of this kind. But true grandeur is unmistakable. It gives you a sense of lift-off that is nearly physical in its pleasure, as if you had been granted the power of flight.

Intimacy can also be faked, or misused, or misunderstood. Contrary to expectations, it does not automatically accompany the use of the first-person voice: plenty of people, including literary characters, do not know themselves well enough to reveal their intimate natures. Nor will its appearance necessarily involve prurient or ugly details, though an intimate tone is certainly better at dealing with that side of life than the grand manner is. Intimacy doesn't have to peer into anyone's well-kept secrets to be deserving of the name. But it does need to give us a sense that we have seen the inside of *something*, and that something needs to strike us as real.

If grandeur gains its power by lifting us above or behind the scenery of daily life, intimacy derives its strength by focusing on that very dailiness. It cares about the ordinary, the routine, the unattended to. It takes another look, a closer look, at the things we knew but had forgotten about, and in place of grandeur's panoramic or telescopic view, it gives us, not the microscopic examination—because that would be too reduced, too divorced from the human in the other direction—but the personal, knowing glance that passes between one set of eyes and another when wordless understanding takes place.

Intimacy in literature can also be wordless, but it relies on language to set it up. The intimacy may dwell in the words of the characters, as in that birthday exchange between Antony and Cleopatra, or it may be carried by the narrator's voice; especially in the novel, it often does both. The novel is by definition an intimate form, with its prolonged private communion between reader and writer, its almost magical capacity to penetrate other minds (a magic that we have learned, over the centuries, to take for granted). But even novels can aim primarily at grandeur. And most good novels will combine at least some degree of grandeur—in their complicated architectural structure, say, or in their contemplative, reflective language—with the intimacy that is their more natural function.

Perhaps by now it is beginning to occur to you that my terms have their antecedents in other opposing pairs. What I am calling grandeur could be connected with tragedy, idealism, the sublime, the godlike. Intimacy could then be made to correspond with comedy, realism, the quotidian, and the earthily human. But does this alignment really work? You can already see that although the pairs may at first seem to divide up in an orderly fashion, they actually, when bunched together, overflow their respective containers. For instance, comedy and realism needn't have a lot to do with each other (Zola amply proves that, with his bleak views of the underside of Parisian life), while the sublime can occur in all sorts of dark, low, earthy places (as it does in the Indian slums of Rohinton Mistry's *A Fine Balance*, or the Australian outback of David Malouf's *The Great World*). So there is something wrong with the old terms, or maybe just with the way they've been used. Literature does not lend itself to being corralled, and these older labels have come down to us largely as material for constructing fences.

Most readers don't, in any case, categorize literature as they read. They enter into the individual work and follow the path it leads them on. I propose to do something like that now, scrutinizing the different approaches taken by a few grandly intimate (or intimately grand) works of poetry, fiction, and nonfiction. But first, let me ask a basic question: Why do we even *want* a work of literature to be grand or intimate? Why not just settle for having things their normal size? Why do we need the sudden and vehement contrast in scale?

It's easier to show this with intimacy, because that is something we think we all desire. But regular life, as it happens, is constructed in a way that makes true intimacy difficult. We do not like to tell uncomfortable truths to other people we know, even the people we are close to. We do not like to see inside the minds of people when they are thinking their most horrifying thoughts (and even the most normal people think horrifying thoughts at times). We prefer, quite often, to skate along on the surface—not because we are superficial, but because we just need to get through life, and observing every moment to its utmost is no way to do that. It takes a literary work, sometimes, to force us to peer closely at human behavior, to consider slowly and seriously why people act the way they do, toward each other and toward themselves. Perhaps this is why so many of Freud's sources were works of literature: he knew that he could most easily locate intimate truths in the pages of fiction and fantasy, in Sophocles' wrenching Oedipus story and in Shakespeare's emotionally complicated plays.

But having looked at ordinary human behavior in this minute fashion, we then need some reassurance that life is not all a matter of gut-searing honesty bubbling to the surface, or selfishness, blind desire, and secret wishes motivating what appear to be normal interchanges. We want the truth, but we also want it made beautiful—not in a way that falsifies the truth, but in a way that makes us able to accept it, by allowing us to see its messiness as part of some larger order. That, I think, is where the grandeur of literature comes in. It makes us believe, despite our practical experience to the contrary, in the superhuman capacities of human beings; it gives us a sense that our species can sometimes transcend life's randomness. We all need to feel this at times, even (or especially) the irreligious among us. Literary grandeur gives us something to admire, something that seems larger than just our petty selves, and admiration is a feeling we cannot live without, however much we may think we can.

The canvas need not be large to support the panoramic or telescopic vision. A tiny lyric poem can combine the grand with the intimate in a way that is as effective (if not, obviously, as prolonged) as a full-scale play or novel. Take, for example, two of the poets I mentioned earlier in this book, Emily Dickinson and Gerard Manley Hopkins. The intimacy of their tone is self-evident. In reading them, we hear ourselves addressed from so close a distance that we hardly even seem to be a "you" to these speakers—more like a second, interior "I."

And yet the material these poems deal with is so powerful, so stirring, that a sense of grandeur enters in. "The Soul selects her own Society— / Then shuts the Door" begins one of Dickinson's most memorable twelve-line poems. You can almost hear the door shutting, in the abrupt two-beat line that follows the more leisurely four- or five-beat opening. It is through the action of closing out the world—firmly, rhythmically, precisely—that Dickinson lifts her poems up to the level at which we seem to be gaining access to more than just ourselves. More than just *her* self too: there is something profoundly impersonal about Dickinson's Soul. At the same

time, the voice in which it is transmitted to us remains idiosyncratic, recognizable. The distinction between personal
and impersonal falls away.

The poets in whom I clearly discern the transcendence I
am calling "grandeur" are for the most part authors with a
religious streak. Strangely, their religiosity does not put me off;
it's as if the poetry itself manages to explain religion to me,
or make spiritual belief palatable, or at least lend it a meaning
I can grasp with my secular mind. And sometimes their
poems even address the exact idea I'm blindly groping toward here—the way in which the grand and the intimate can
coexist, so that each is manifested in the other. Here, for instance, is Hopkins on this very subject:

> As kingfishers catch fire, dragonflies draw flame;
>   As tumbled over rim in roundy wells
>   Stones ring; like each tucked string tells, each hung bell's
> Bow swung finds tongue to fling out broad its name;
> Each mortal thing does one thing and the same:
>   Deals out that being indoors each one dwells;
>   Selves—goes itself; *myself* it speaks and spells,
> Crying *Whát I dó is me: for that I came.*
>
> I say móre: the just man justices;
>   Keeps gráce: thát keeps all his goings graces;
> Acts in God's eye what in God's eye he is—
>   Chríst. For Christ plays in ten thousand places,
> Lovely in limbs, and lovely in eyes not his
>   To the Father through the features of men's faces.

The language itself is grand, with its tolling alliterations
and internal rhymes—proof in itself, it would seem, that each
thing can find "tongue to fling out broad its name." This is
onomatopoeia raised to a philosophical level: the words sound
not just like their alluded-to natural noises, but like the em-

bodiment of the poem's central idea, the notion that each "deals out that being indoors each one dwells." It is also grammar stretched nearly to its breaking point. Odd inversions abound. The word "Selves," in the seventh line, actually functions as a verb before it retreats into a pair of echoing pronouns. Meanwhile, the play back and forth between "I" and "Christ," "God" and "myself" is so fraught and strenuous that the profession of deep faith almost verges on blasphemy. We and the dragonflies exist because God made us, yes, but He is only visible through our faces and their wings and everything else in nature. Everyman is Christ, and every self—even inhuman selves, even *insentient* selves, like stones and bells—has something divine about it. This, I feel, is a religion one can live with. (Though apparently the Church fathers of the poet's own time felt otherwise: they instructed Hopkins to stop publishing his strange poetry and he, as a good Jesuit priest, obeyed.)

Religious grandeur, or grandeur that draws on religious principles, naturally takes a different form in the novel. Consider *The Brothers Karamazov*. All of Dostoyevsky's works are tinged to some degree with religious belief, even where, as in a character like *Crime and Punishment*'s murderous Raskolnikov or *Demons*' rule-defying Stavrogin, it takes the form of a willful resistance to belief. But in *The Brothers Karamazov* Christianity takes center stage from the very beginning of the book. When we first meet Alyosha, the youngest and by far the most saintly of the three brothers, he is living at a monastery, trying to determine whether the religious life is the right one for him. He also seems to be searching for hidden truths that he hopes may lie behind the ugliness of daily life. (As the motherless child of the boorish Fyodor Karamazov, not to mention the sibling of the violent-tempered Dmitri and the cold, calculating Ivan, Alyosha has more reasons than most for finding it ugly.)

This is a novel in which the family members have conversations like:

"Alyoshka, is there a God?"
   "There is."
   "And is there immortality, Ivan? At least some kind, at least a little, a teeny-tiny one?"
   "There is no immortality either."
   "Not of any kind?"
   "Not of any kind."
   "Complete zero? Or is there something? Maybe there's some kind of something? At least not nothing!"
   "Complete zero."
   "Alyoshka, is there immortality?"
   "There is."
   "Both God and immortality?"
   "Both God and immortality. Immortality is in God."
   "Hm. More likely Ivan is right . . ."

It is a novel in which the entirety of Book VI, amounting to more than fifty pages of text, is devoted to a summary of the life and teachings of Father Zosima, Alyosha's revered instructor. And it is also the novel in which one whole chapter, a frequently excerpted chapter called "The Grand Inquisitor," consists of a strange, fable-like digression about the nature and intensity of faith in the sixteenth century. That this story-within-a-story is actually a "poem" made up and recited by the irreligious Ivan only complicates the novel's many-layered complexity and ambiguity.

Still, even the bits of dialogue I've quoted above suggest how an intimate, individually inflected tone can be intermingled with these grand topics. In contrast to, say, Shakespeare's characters—or even Henry James's—Dostoyevsky's people speak, for the most part, in mundane language. They repeat themselves and stumble over phrases and get things wrong and change their minds midstream. And the oddest thing is that even Dostoyevsky's *narrator* speaks to us in this personal, slightly bumbling manner. "Alexei Fyodorovich Karamazov was the third son of a landowner from our district, Fyodor Pavlovich Karamazov," the novel begins,

> well known in his day (and still remembered among us) because of his dark and tragic death, which happened exactly thirteen years ago and which I shall speak of in its proper place. For the moment I will only say of this "landowner" (as we used to call him, though for all his life he hardly ever lived on his estate) that he was a strange type, yet one rather frequently met with, precisely the type of man who is not only worthless and depraved but muddleheaded as well—one of those muddleheaded people who still handle their own little business deals quite skillfully, if nothing else.

This narrator flits in and out of the story, occasionally reminding us of his presence, more often hiding in the woodwork, and at times conveying to us extremely private scenes at which he couldn't possibly have been present if he is indeed, as he purports to be, a real person from "our district" and not a disembodied, all-seeing author. I have not yet decided, even for myself, what effect this narrator has on the relative grandeur or intimacy of Dostoyevsky's tales (for he is there in some of the other novels too, in *Demons* and *The Idiot* and perhaps in others I haven't yet read). Does his decidedly human and often inept presence make the novel more graspable by turning it into a kind of conversation between him and us? Or does the fact that his views are so partial and conscribed paradoxically allow the whole work to transcend itself, giving us the feeling that the tale is bigger than its teller, more complicated than he could ever understand? *Both,* I want to say, if that is not too evasive; and even then I am not sure that these two options cover all the ground.

This linguistic intimacy, significant as it is, is not the only kind Dostoyevsky practices. The points at which *The Brothers Karamazov* moves closest to us—indeed, grabs us by the throat and practically squeezes the life out of us—tend to be moments where plot is used to sound the depths of personality. These events, most of them sidelines to the major progress of the story, occur to and among the characters, allowing us to see how they respond to each other, or rather, how they actually *become* themselves in reaction to each other, so that our knowledge of them, like their own knowledge of themselves, is unexpected, sudden, and conditional.

One of the most striking examples of this is an encounter between Alyosha and some practically nameless characters who have been humiliated by his brother Dmitri. (They do have names, but one can never remember them: that's how minor they are, in the overall story.) It begins when Alyosha runs across a group of boys who are throwing rocks at each other. Their primary victim—whom he intervenes to save, and who bites him in return—is a boy that the other schoolboys relentlessly tease with the word "whiskbroom." When Alyosha pursues the story, he learns that they are derisively referring to the broom-like beard worn by the boy's father, an impoverished former captain in the Russian infantry (and, not incidentally, one of those embarrassing, ludicrously unrestrained figures in which Dostoyevsky's fiction abounds). It was this beard, this whiskbroom of a beard, that Dmitri Karamazov grabbed in order to drag the captain out of a tavern into the public square, an insult that occurred just as all the schoolboys, including the man's own son, were passing by. "When he saw me in such a state, sir," the captain tells Alyosha, "he rushed up to me: 'Papa!' he cried, 'papa!' He caught hold of me, hugged me, tried to pull me away, crying to my offender: 'Let go, let go, it's my papa, my papa, forgive him'—that was what he cried: 'Forgive him!' And he took hold of him, too, with his little hands, and kissed his hand, that very hand, sir."

Alyosha responds to this tale of terrible humiliation—the father's humiliation by Dmitri, and the boy's even more intense shame on his father's behalf—by promising to obtain an apology from his brother. Then, as if in a separate gesture, but in recompense for the same deed, he offers the captain some financial assistance from Dmitri's fiancée. The captain at first accepts the money in amazement ("Is this for me, sir, so much money, two hundred roubles? Good heavens! But I haven't seen so much money for the past four years") and goes on at great length about all the things he will now be able to do for his family that he could not afford to do before. But then, in that sudden way Dostoyevsky characters have of turning on a dime, he reverses himself and throws the money back at Alyosha.

> "Report to those who sent you that the whiskbroom does not sell his honor!" he cried out, raising his hands in the air . . . "And what would I tell my boy, if I took money from you for our disgrace?" And having said this, he broke into a run, this time without turning around. Alyosha looked after him with inexpressible sadness. Oh, he understood that the captain had not known until the very last moment that he would crumple the bills and fling them down.

It has taken me a long time to convey the bare details of this scene, and yet I have left out all that was most important: in particular, the prolonged way in which the captain brought out the story of his humiliation, the verbosity of both his self-abasement and his gratitude when he first received the two hundred roubles, the detailed extremity of his actions when he threw them down. And behind all this lies Alyosha's encounter with the boy himself (who bit him, it turns out, because he was Dmitri's brother), so that the father's speeches, foolish and embarrassing as they are, only intensify our sense of the boy's own unspoken feelings, his own terrible victimization. It is all incredibly painful, and the whole encounter seems to occur at a pace slower than real time. Dostoyevsky lengthens every horrifying second, making us feel that the scene will never end, that we will never get away from this reflected, refracted pain. It is unendurable, and yet he forces us to endure it.

Why *do* we endure it? Well, some of us don't; there are many people who can't stomach Dostoyevsky, who argue that he wallows in emotional pain and overemphasizes the melodrama of life. I understand the position, but I can't imagine sharing it. For me, the excesses of Dostoyevsky's world *are* real life, more real than anything I usually encounter in my own routine existence, or at any rate more transparent. By combining grandeur and intimacy in precisely the way he does, Dostoyevsky somehow overcomes my resistance sufficiently to make me see life as it is. It is only there, on the page with him, that I can slow experience down enough to grasp it fully. It is only there that I can begin to perceive how many sides every personality has, or see how degradation and exaltation can be paired in a single human soul.

If Christianity was Dostoyevsky's religion, art was Henry James's. His prevailing attitude toward this source of grandeur was a very typical mixture (typical of him, I mean) of doubt and faith, and he tended to lend the same combination of dubiousness and hope to his more sentient characters. They have a habit, these Jamesian contemplatives, of overvaluing "the beautiful," even as they also find themselves reconsidering its worth at every turn.

Here is a pertinent bit of conversation from *The Tragic Muse*, where James is relaying to us a discussion that takes place in Paris between Gabriel Nash, a writer and aesthete, and Nick Dormer, an aspiring painter. As the two of them talk, they wander together through the nighttime streets, so that eventually they come up against one of the city's major monuments:

> "Don't you think your style is a little affected?" Nick asked, laughing, as they proceeded.
>
> "That's always the charge against a personal manner; if you have any at all people think you have too much. Perhaps, perhaps—who can say? Of course one isn't perfect; but that's the delightful thing about art, that there is always more to learn and more to do; one can polish and polish and refine and refine. No doubt I'm rough still, but I'm in the right direction: I make it my business to take for granted an interest in the beautiful."
>
> "Ah, the beautiful—there it stands, over there!" said Nick Dormer. "I am not so sure about yours—I don't know what I've got hold of. But Notre Dame *is* solid; Notre Dame *is* wise; on Notre Dame the distracted mind can rest. Come over and look at her!"

It is the enduring aesthetic value of this architectural wonder, as opposed to the possibly temporary value of his own work and Gabriel's, that compels Nick at this particular juncture, just as it is the building's blessed impersonality that stands in such contrast to the suspect "personal manner." The fact that Notre Dame is a great cathedral is not merely coincidental here, but nor does that function, its purely religious function, account for Nick's attitude. He is responding to the building as a work of art, a beautiful thing on which his artist's eye can rest, and the fact that its beauties were created in the service of God is not at the forefront of his "distracted" mind. His casual blasphemy, his perhaps-too-easy intimacy with that which is meant to resist intimacy, is most apparent in his use of the feminine pronoun in the phrase "Come over and look at her!" It is a pronoun that cannot be justified, at least in English, by the fact that Our Lady is female; the tone, in Nick's wording, is what one might use of something smaller-scale than a cathedral, something like a portrait in a museum. In his very effort to praise the grand monumentality of the building, he is also reducing it to something closer to his own size.

The notion that a lasting and significant work of art can be a "she" carries special weight in a novel whose title, *The Tragic Muse*, refers to an actual woman, a young and talented actress named Miriam Rooth. This is a novel, moreover, in which the central characters spend a lot of time worrying over the question of whether the theater—that most ephemeral and personal of art forms, embodied as it is in the gestures and voices of individual actors—can truly be considered a transcendent art. The novel does not make up its mind (James's novels rarely do), but it remains persistently interested in the apparent paradoxes raised by the pursuit of this question. Is it the personal that moves us and makes us susceptible to art, or does art have to be larger than the merely personal to be great? Does the actor's art lean more toward grandeur or toward intimacy, or are they even separable, on the stage? Are portraits a low form of painting simply because they portray the human countenance, or does that give them the highest claim to our interest, both aesthetic and emotional? What about novels in this regard, specifically the novel we hold in our hands? Is *The Tragic Muse* aiming at the solidity and wisdom of Notre Dame, and if not, in what sense are we justified in calling it art? All this and more is encapsulated and foreshadowed in that little conversation between Gabriel Nash and Nick Dormer.

That Gabriel Nash does indeed have an affected style—as a person and, we presume, as an artist—definitely enters into the equation here. He may share his author's profession and, it would seem, some of his professed attitudes, but he is also one of the more questionable figures in the book. Yet his affectation alone is not enough to damn him as an artist. The tragic muse herself is a bundle of affectations, but she knows better than anyone around her how to convey the appearance, the sensation of truth—which, on the stage, *is* truth. In the same way, Henry James's style, affected as it may seem when excerpted elsewhere, creates within his own novels both a coherent world and a coherent worldview. Immersed in *The Tragic Muse*, one is likely to feel that *only* such a style, with all its quirky hesitations and exaggerations, is adequate to the complex truths that James finds himself repeatedly pursuing.

Part of James's style, like part of Dostoyevsky's, lies in the creation of a personal narrator, a figure who at times enters the tale and addresses us as an individual. James's nearly invisible storyteller makes his presence felt mainly by interjecting phrases like "I hasten to add" into his sentences, or referring to one or another of the characters as "our friend." At the end, though, he positively steps from behind the arras and announces:

> These matters are highly recent however, as I say; so that in glancing about the little circle of the interests I have tried to evoke I am suddenly warned by a sharp sense of modernness. This renders it difficult for me, for example, in taking leave of our wonderful Miriam, to do much more than allude to

the general impression that her remarkable career is even
yet only in its early prime.

The tone is personal and individual, as in Dostoyevsky.
But whereas Dostoyevsky's intermittent narrator is a limited
and somewhat humorless figure, James's is much more like his
author: witty, worldly, and generously polite, in that he presumes a fair measure of wit and worldliness in us. If he takes
toward his characters a slightly amused, detached view, compounded of tolerance for their perceived foibles and affection
for their evident charms, that is not so different from the view
he takes of himself—or, for that matter, the rest of humanity,
which we can assume includes us. His attitude toward his own
omniscience is ambiguous. He professes an inability to tell us
everything about which we might be curious, and at the same
time admits he has special funds of knowledge that he can, on
occasion, disperse. The intimacy of his voice suggests that he,
we, and his characters all exist on the same plane, and yet the
slight archness of his tone implies something else. It hints that
there is some kind of collusion going on here—though
whether the forces joined together are the fictional (his and
the characters') or the real (his and ours) remains impossible
to tell.

In general, for a novelist to emerge from behind his curtain
and speak to us in his own voice seems the most intimate of
gestures. Presumably that's why the "Dear Reader" approach
was invented in the first place: to give the audience a sense
that it was being personally spoken to, guided through the
fictional maze by an understanding and intelligent friend.
There are cases, though, in which the emergence of this
voice has exactly the opposite effect. In those cases (and per-

haps they are more frequent than I imagine), the palpable and self-confessed presence of an author is *itself* the signal of a move toward transcendence or grandeur. It is at such moments that the roof lifts off the novel, and we are suddenly rocketed up to the capacious heights of the author's own viewpoint.

I'm thinking now of a passage that occurs in *The Family Mashber*, the marvelous Yiddish novel by the Russian-Jewish writer who called himself Der Nister. That pen name, which means "The Hidden One" in Yiddish, was the pseudonym adopted by the fiction writer, translator, journalist, and critic Pinhas Kahanovitch, who was born in the Ukraine in 1884 and who, as a young man, took part in the modernist movement that briefly flourished in Kiev in the 1920s. *The Family Mashber*, completed when he was fifty-five, is the only book of his I've read, and it's a very strange novel indeed: a kind of massively elongated folktale, a seven-hundred-page shaggy dog story set in the Pale of Settlement and populated almost entirely by Jews. Landed aristocrats, Cossacks, and other Christians exist around the edges, but they barely function in the plot, which for the most part concerns the pettinesses and machinations, though also the occasional concessions and kindnesses, of one of the principal merchant families within a Jewish village.

For the first hundred or so pages, practically all you get is a mass of anthropological and folkloric detail. You keep reading because the detail is interesting and the emerging cast of characters is beginning to take shape, but you have no idea where, if anywhere, this is all going to take you. And then at a certain point, just after we've been introduced to Alter, the third Mashber brother—"more a misfortune than he was a brother," with his simpleton's smile and his strangely unnerving gaze—we are suddenly accosted by a previously indiscernible narrator. "And here we must interrupt our narrative," he interjects,

> in order to say a few words about Alter and his biography.
> It may be that this is not the place for him, and it may
> be that generally speaking there ought not to be a place here
> for someone like him who does not—who cannot—take an
> active part in the narrative, and we might simply have passed
> him over or mentioned him only occasionally here and there.
> But we have not done that, and after much consideration
> we have introduced him here and we mean to occupy our-
> selves with him for a little while longer because, although
> he does not play an active role, still, it is a role, if only be-
> cause he existed and because he existed in the household
> about which we have been speaking, and since blood is
> thicker than water, and because we have in mind the re-
> searcher who two or three generations from now may find
> in later members of the family a tiny kernel of that sickly
> inheritance which in the generation being discussed here
> was unhappily Alter's portion.

From here on the narrator stays with us, making his presence felt, not continuously, but at occasional important junc-
tures, when he offers us useful bits of commentary and
information just as we are likely to want or need them. And
now we realize that exactly this—the outside perspective, the
cool authorial distance—was what was lacking in the novel
up to that point. The claustrophobic sense of enclosure, realistic as it was, had almost begun to stifle us. This new
viewpoint is not utterly alien, for the narrator too seems to
be Jewish, as evidenced by his speech rhythms, his local
prejudices, his choice of phrases. But unlike the other characters, he is not completely confined by the world of the tale.
He, at least, seems to know where we are going, to have an
idea about what is pertinent and what is not. We are reassured

by the sense that what we are letting ourselves in for is not just anecdote, but art.

Of course, the intrusive tale-teller does not give us this feeling of reassurance on his own; it is the existence of an author clever enough to invent this narrator that wins us over. Doubly clever, really: to invent such a narrator, and then to withhold him for a hundred pages until we are desperate for his services. This is an author who will be able to guide us toward something worth having. He has, as it were, the necessary authority. At the same time, he appears to be wise enough to know the limits of his own authority, his own cleverness, for he is already thinking of the world that will come "two or three generations from now," when he is no longer there to control it.

Some works of literature are born with a sense of tragic grandeur, while others have it thrust upon them through the permutations of history. *The Family Mashber* has both qualities. When Der Nister finished the book in 1939, the old Jewish life of the *shtetl* had already vanished, and, as his preface makes clear, "It has not been easy for me to evoke that world, to animate it and to put its people into motion." So his novel, even when it was new, had its own tragic shadow cast over it. But the author had no way of knowing, when he finished this first volume, that he would never be allowed to complete the multivolume work he had undertaken. He could not foresee that he would die in a Soviet prison hospital in 1950, having been arrested as part of Stalin's campaign against "rootless cosmopolitans." And he could not have known, in 1939, that the idea of a lost Jewish world would soon take on another and even darker meaning. So the final lines of his novel have for us a sadness and a resonance that even he, great writer that he was, could not have put into them:

> Well, that's it. And now we take the narrative back from
> Mayerl and we undertake to report what is to come in our
> own fashion and in the style that is unique to ourselves.
>   Again, that's it. And with this, we believe that our first
> book is finished.

To be deprived of a promised sequel—to lose the characters
midway through their fates—is always hard. But in this case
the loss is compounded by history. We, looking back, have
our own special and additional reasons for feeling anguished
that the first book was also the last.

Let me say a word, here, about Jews and history. Perhaps
my perspective is distorted by the fact that I am a secular Jew
myself, so you may want to discount my notion accordingly.
But it seems to me that while the tragedy of Christianity is
inherent in its religious doctrine—the fall of Man, the redemption through the death of Christ—the tragedy of the
Jews lies much more in their relation to history. So when
what I am calling grandeur, which could be another word for
tragedy, appears in literary works with Christian leanings, it
is likely to have an abstract and theological aspect; whereas
when it appears in Jewish literature, it is more likely to draw
on events that have actually happened in the world, either the
world *within* the literary work or the known, historical world
outside it. I grant that I may be wrong about this. There is
certainly quite a lot of Jewish literature I haven't read (as
there is also a lot of Christian literature I haven't read). But if
I just compare the works I have loved in the two categories,
this difference seems to hold true.

At any rate, if history, and in particular the tragic history
of the Jews, can lend added richness to a work of great literary merit like *The Family Mashber*, it can also give a kind of
novelistic power even to a book that was never intended as

literature in the first place. This is what happened to Victor Klemperer's wartime diaries. Published in an English translation under the title *I Will Bear Witness*, these diaries chronicle the weekly, sometimes daily existence of a Dresden-based professor of German literature in the period 1933 to 1945. That Klemperer was a non-practicing Jew with an "Aryan" wife is the plot, so to speak, of his account of life in Hitler's Germany. He watches as one friend or relative after another flees the country, but he—devoted to the German language, unable to imagine life elsewhere, and convinced until far too late in the day that his marriage to a non-Jew (not to mention his own merely nominal Jewishness) will protect him—stays put. As each year passes, his life becomes more and more constricted. First he loses his job, then his car, then the right to own a house in the countryside and even the right to keep pets. Eventually he is forced to wear a yellow star, and when his wife refuses to divorce him, they are both moved into a cramped, crowded "Jewish house," where life, tentative and fearful, is carried on at poverty's edge. And then, after he has already received his transport orders, mere days before he is due to be shipped out to a death camp, Dresden is bombed by the Allies, and in the ensuing confusion Klemperer and his wife escape.

Unlike Der Nister, Klemperer is not a brilliant writer, and in any case this is a diary, not necessarily meant for other eyes. His style is plodding; his concerns are often petty or pedantic. We do not warm to him, because he has neither the willingness nor the ability to charm. But his story is gripping, in part *because* of the plodding and the pettiness. This is normal life, gradually becoming less normal as each year passes. The minutiae of Klemperer's existence form the basis of our intimacy with him—not an emotional intimacy such as you might form with another person, but an experiential intimacy such as you have with yourself. In a sense we *are* him, and in another sense we remain completely separate, because we know what is coming whereas he does not. For anyone who recalls the salient fact about Dresden's twentieth-century history—the firebombing of 1945—the diary is like two competing stories racing toward each other at different speeds. On the one hand there is Klemperer's achingly slow life, with its gradual, steady decline, and on the other hand there is this gigantic historical event hurtling toward him. That the terrible bombing, in destroying his city, saves rather than kills him is only part of the book's tremendous irony. Peering through the lens of history, we are enabled to be two sizes at once: the antlike creature blindly moving forward on the ground, and the godlike overseer waiting for the inevitable explosion. It is a remarkable experience, and I have rarely in my reading life felt such suspense.

A similar sense of history inflects Edmund de Waal's unusual family memoir, *The Hare with Amber Eyes*, but here the dual perspective is self-consciously built into the account from the beginning, not forced on it by subsequent events. Plotting is both a given and an invented feature of this book. In its broader outlines, the nonfiction story has been handed to de Waal; he cannot make things up. And yet the very way in which he chooses to dole out the information he has painstakingly gathered lends a true sense of mystery to the work. Because he is dealing only with his own family history, it might seem that the author runs the risk of portraying massive world events through a Lilliputian telescope. Luckily, the family in question occupied an oddly central position in the history of several European countries. Even more luckily, de Waal is the kind of nonfiction writer who only comes along a few times in every decade, a person highly sensitive to nuance and form. (He is a ceramicist by profession, as it happens, but—or and—he writes better than most professional novelists.)

His story begins with several visits to Japan, where Edmund, the English son of a half-Dutch Anglican clergyman, goes to learn his trade. There he becomes acquainted with his Great-Uncle Iggie (his actual name is Ignace Ephrussi), an elderly gay man who has lived in Japan for many years with his younger Japanese partner. Iggie owns a remarkable collection of 264 Japanese netsuke, but what is most remarkable, perhaps, is that he owned them *before* he ever got to Japan. In fact, these small, expertly designed, witty but beautiful Japanese objects—each tiny enough to be held in the palm of one's hand and valuable enough to be displayed in a museum—have been handed down in the Ephrussi family since the late nineteenth century. Edmund, who is told by his great-uncle that he will eventually inherit the collection, decides to look into its history.

The original collector was Charles Ephrussi, part of the Paris branch of this international Jewish banking clan, which seems to have been second in wealth and importance only to the Rothschilds, with whom the Ephrussis occasionally intermarried. Having spread out from Odessa to Vienna and Paris, the Ephrussis quickly acquired enough polish to spawn art collectors as well as bankers, and Charles, who was apparently a fine amateur art critic as well as an early exponent of *japonisme*, was perhaps the most artistic of the lot. A dandy and a boulevardier, he was friends with Manet, Pissarro, Degas, and Proust; he also hobnobbed with French aristocrats, until he fell out with them over the Dreyfus affair. In 1899, a few years before his own death, Charles gave his netsuke collection as a wedding present to his younger cousin Viktor, a member of the Vienna branch of the family.

So now the tiny objects move, in their fancy display case,

to the center of Freud's, Schnitzler's, Wittgenstein's, and Karl Kraus's world. The vitrine occupies the dressing room of Viktor's wife, Emmy, where the children, including the young Iggie, are allowed to play with the valuable netsuke— the hare with amber eyes, the monk bent over his begging dish, the various kinds of fruit and vegetables, creatures and humans and objects—as if they were merely toys. And there they remain, through all the vicissitudes of the first third of the twentieth century, until the family finally flees Vienna in 1938.

By this time the reader will have become so caught up in the story that she will have neglected to ask herself a crucial question: given that all the household furnishings had to be left behind, how did the netsuke eventually end up in Iggie's hands? It is precisely by holding this information in reserve—by distracting us, as a magician would, so that we don't even wonder about it until he is ready to spring the answer on us—that de Waal achieves one of his most masterful effects. For it turns out that the Ephrussi family had an Austrian servant named Anna (we don't even know her last name) who stayed behind in Vienna and kept working for a while at the requisitioned mansion. Gradually she smuggled all of the netsuke out of the building in her pockets, a few at a time, and hid them in her mattress, where they stayed for the duration of the war. After the war was over, she eventually succeeded in returning the collection to its rightful owners.

A tiny, beautiful object—even 264 tiny, beautiful objects—cannot begin to replace all the lives and ideals that were lost in those years, and in that place. But something about this tale of selfless generosity restores, in quite a visceral and moving way, one's faith in human nature. It sometimes lies in the power of art to make the small stand in for the large, to give us an object we can hold in our hands and make us feel we are holding the world. *The Hare with Amber Eyes* possesses that power.

It also turns out that de Waal's book has a built-in connection with literary history, for Charles Ephrussi, that netsuke-collecting ancestor, was one of the primary models for Proust's Charles Swann. The parallels are obvious, and numerous. Swann was an assimilated Jew who managed to penetrate the highest circles of French aristocratic society, and so was Ephrussi. Both men wrote art historical essays—Swann about Vermeer, Ephrussi about Dürer. Each had a beautiful, willful mistress who adorned herself in Japanese kimonos. And so on. Charles Ephrussi, of course, was real, and Charles Swann merely a fiction; yet it is Swann who is, and will always remain, the larger, more memorable character. This is not de Waal's fault. Scrupulously reported reality cannot compare with an imagination the size of Proust's. *Think you there was or might be such a man as this I dreamt of? Gentle madam, no.*

Perhaps it will seem perverse of me to compare Swann, even implicitly, with Antony. As tragic lovers they have almost nothing in common. It is only by a linguistic stretch that we can even call Swann heroic, for his is the very subdued heroism of the modern protagonist: a largely honorable existence led within a society that mainly values the appearance of honor over the thing itself. And if Swann is admirable, he is also pathetic, for he is reduced to terrible self-deceptions and ridiculous concessions by his love for the unworthy Odette. We never pity Antony in the way we pity Swann, for Antony is in love with someone who is at least his equal (an impossible achievement, in Proust's world). On the other hand, we never really understand Antony in the way we grow to understand Swann. And that intense, relentless degree of understanding—of investigation into the very process of understanding—turns out to be one of Proust's greatest literary strengths.

Remembrance of Things Past, or *In Search of Lost Time,* or whatever they decide to call it in the decades and centuries to come, is a work that breaks wide open my distinction between grandeur and intimacy. There is no single part of this many-volumed novel that you can point to and say, "Here it is grand," or "Here it becomes intimate." The whole thing is grand and intimate at once. Every one of those sentences that last a page, or paragraphs that go on for the length of a normal author's chapter, is focused minutely on the interior details of a quietly led day-to-day existence. And yet the cumulative experience is that of contemplating, not just an individual life, not even a single society's life (though it is all these things too), but Time itself: its slow and fast passage, its retrieval through memory and history, its disappearance in death. You reach the end of this massive reading project, through which you have crept at a snail's pace—moment by moment, year by year, as time elapses both inside and outside the novel—and you feel you have arrived somewhere. It is not precisely a place within yourself, but nor is it completely outside yourself. It is an Elsewhere made accessible to you through the efforts of another imagination, collaborating for a time with your own.

SIX

ELSEWHERE

To be honest, I have not actually read the undulating sentences and endless paragraphs of *A la recherche du temps perdu.* What I have read are their successive English versions. It is a bit like Zeno's paradox, this journey that approaches nearer and nearer to the thing itself without ever fully arriving. It began in my very late teens, when I first attempted C. K. Scott Moncrieff's translation of *Remembrance of Things Past* in the seven-volume pastel-colored paperback edition. That time, I foundered on the closely printed pages of *Swann's Way.* Later, in my twenties and early thirties, I made my way through the silver-and-black volumes of Terence Kilmartin's intelligent and clarifying revision of Scott Moncrieff, which still carried the Shakespearean title. And then much later still—nearing sixty, and thus older than most of the white-haired characters who attend that ghoulish party in the novel's final section—I once again went through all seven books, this time using D. J. Enright's fine completion of Kilmartin's and Scott Moncrieff's work, now retitled *In Search of Lost Time.* Each time, I would have described what I was doing as "reading Proust," but I am sure any French-speaker would have begged to disagree.

I may be an avid reader, but I am also an appallingly mono-lingual one. The English language is the golden prison I in-habit: richly and divertingly adorned, but with all the exits closed off, preventing me from making my escape to French or Russian or Italian or German. Only the Spanish door is slightly ajar, but its opening is just barely wide enough for me to peek through longingly. That is, I can read a novel in Span-ish if I'm desperate, but I will get far more out of it if I read the same thing rendered in someone else's English.

Because of this handicap, I am dependent on the work of translators; they are the kind emissaries, you might say, who bring news of the outside world to my cell. I could dispense with these do-gooders, I suppose, if I chose to read only works written originally in English, and I *did* so choose, during a brief period of callow youthfulness. But even the great out-pouring of nineteenth-century English fiction can seem insufficient and tedious after a while, and if you start ven-turing into the twentieth century, particularly the late twentieth century, you will soon find yourself in need of foreign companionship.

So rather than resent my helpers, I have come to feel a deep affection for these selfless workers, these brilliant shad-ows, these people whose highest aim is to remain at the very margin of visibility. No translator wants his achievement stolen or denied, yet just as certainly, no translator wants her voice to overpower that of her source author. It's a very care-ful balance. And however well the disappearing act is done, something of the translator's own sensibility invariably enters into the work we're given in English.

This is not to say that a Margaret Jull Costa translation of Eça de Queirós sounds like a Margaret Jull Costa trans-lation of Javier Marías; not at all. If it did, Jull Costa would have failed in her primary aim, which is to let us hear the writer's voice as she herself hears it in the original Portuguese or Spanish. I want to stress that word "hear." The way Margaret Jull Costa works, I gather, is that she reads aloud every sentence of every translation she produces—the hundreds of pages of Eça de Queirós's *The Maias*, the thousands of pages of Javier Marías's *Your Face Tomorrow*, the novels, essays, and stories of José Saramago, Teolinda Gersão, Bernardo Atxaga, and others—to test its sound in her actual ear as well as her internal one. What she is listening for is not just the musicality of the English line, though she demands that, too; she is searching as well for an echo, a correspondence between her formulations in English and the author's voice as it comes across in his own language. These correspondences are a matter of rhythm, of punctuation, of diction, of sentence structure, but they are also something more elusive and mysterious than that. The American writer Leonard Michaels used to say about his own short stories that when he finally got a sentence to *sound* right to his ear, he knew he had solved the problem of meaning. Margaret Jull Costa uses a similar standard when she brings forth the writing of others, and her quiet genius lies in her ability to repeatedly transform her own authorial voice into the recognizable voice of someone else.

Yet she never disappears completely. Something of her own character must remain embedded in the lines, however tenuously, for the translation to be persuasive, for it to feel like the work of an individual rather than a conglomerate or a machine. This is why a Margaret Jull Costa translation of Javier Marías will sound slightly but noticeably different from an Esther Allen translation of Javier Marías. He is clearly the same author in both cases—witty, self-aware, elaborately eloquent, fascinated by sex and violence, immersed in movies and television, drawn to Anglo-American culture, but with a saving distance that makes him seem totally unlike anything we could have produced. (That, after all, is why we go to foreign writers, why we *need* them.) Still, Allen's Marías is not quite Jull Costa's Marías. The difference is so subtle it's hard to define: something to do with Allen's expansive American ear, something to do with Jull Costa's uncanny ability to locate Anglo-Saxon equivalents for Latinate terms. If I were pressed, I would say that Esther Allen's Marías sounds more like a Spaniard, Margaret Jull Costa's more like a native English speaker. Which is preferable? I suppose it depends on what kind of reader you are, or perhaps on which translation you encountered first.

Priority may be what accounts for my allegiance to Michael Hulse as the translator of W. G. Sebald. The first books I read by this postwar German writer (Sebald was born in 1944, and his works all seem to be rooted in the aftermath of the Third Reich) were *The Emigrants* and *The Rings of Saturn*. Both were translated by Hulse, in such a marvelously poetic and yet down-to-earth way that they felt almost like works of English literature. This was especially true of *The Rings of Saturn*, a book built around a walking tour of England and containing numerous references to the English author Sir Thomas Browne, a favorite of Sebald's. The Germanness of the book's narrator was impossible to miss, but it had been transmuted, in Hulse's sinuous sentences, into an Anglo-German melancholic sensibility. In fact, Sebald—who lived more than half his life in England, though he continued to write in his native tongue—may be one of those writers who actually appeals to English readers more than German ones, because he offers us something we Anglophones feel we collectively lack. Whether that is moral seriousness, or endless patience, or an inbred awareness of history, or an almost planetary distance from our daily habits and assumptions, or a deeply secular sense of what you might call original sin, is impossible for me to say; it's probably a combination of all these and other things besides. Whatever it is, it lends Sebald's works in English the kind of estranged pertinence one finds in a book like Penelope Fitzgerald's *The Blue Flower* or Louise Glück's *A Village Life*: pertinent because we feel ourselves to be somehow implicated, yet with a safety net of foreignness that protects us from the author's too-direct glance. It is as if Fitzgerald and Glück, reaching over from English toward something else, have arrived at the same contemplative mid-point that Sebald occupies when his strangely hybrid works— neither fully fictional or nonfictional, but always infused with an uncanny combination of imaginative reconstruction and displayed evidence—are brought into English from German.

At least, this was the feeling I got from those first two Hulse translations. So when I came to *Austerlitz*, translated instead by Anthea Bell, I was startled. I suspect that on some level the Bell translation is as good as the Hulse, but it was nonetheless a barrier I felt I had to overcome, a new voice added to Sebald's old one; my "Sebald," that is, had apparently consisted of Sebald plus Hulse. And there was again the shock of a change when I moved to Michael Hamburger's elegant, attentive translation of Sebald's posthumously published *After Nature*. (Sebald died suddenly at the age of fifty-seven in a car crash near his Norfolk home, and for those of us who had only recently discovered him, it was like losing a new friend.) This time, though, I realized what was happening and was able to brace myself against the unexpected. Also, in the case of *After Nature*—a book-length unrhymed poem, set out on the page in broken lines—I was alert to the way in which the transformation of genre would inevitably mean a transformation of voice. This, I subsequently reasoned, had also been true for *Austerlitz*, which is Sebald's closest thing to a real novel, a sequential story featuring a fictional character other than the narrator. So what I took as a shift attributable to the translators might well have been just as much, or instead, a shift in Sebald's own writing style. In any case, despite the differences I was sensing, Sebald remained essentially Sebald in all his manifestations, for great writers can never escape themselves, whether through translation or through their own development or even through death.

My most intense experience with translation, thus far, has involved a Japanese author. Like Javier Marías and W. G. Sebald, Haruki Murakami is a writer who is intimately acquainted with Anglo-American culture even as he remains outside it. (I think writers of this kind may well make the most interesting test cases for translation; at any rate, I find myself repeatedly drawn to them.) Murakami, who has translated Raymond Carver, F. Scott Fitzgerald, and Paul Theroux into Japanese, is partial to the Beatles, jazz, Scotch whiskey, Marx Brothers movies, and many other products of Western culture. He often injects something akin to an American sensibility—a rebellious, non-salaryman's sensibility—into his hapless fictional protagonists. Yet the novels are written in Japanese and set, for the most part, in Japan, so when we read them in English, we get, as with Marías and Sebald, a strange sensation of foreignness mixed with familiarity, of worlds collapsing in on each other.

The first three novels I read by Murakami—*A Wild Sheep Chase*, *Hard-Boiled Wonderland and the End of the World*, and *Dance Dance Dance*—were all translated by Alfred Birnbaum. When I finished the books, I was mildly curious to know more about Murakami; I was *desperate* to know more about Birnbaum. Who was this guy who could come up with two completely different kinds of English, an old-fashioned fairy-tale diction and a sharp-edged modern idiom, to render the two intertwined plot strands of *Hard-Boiled Wonderland*? How

did he manage to do that weird, youthful, but never annoy-
ingly with-it voice in which Murakami's narrator-protagonists
spoke to themselves? How, in short, could he make a Japanese
writer sound so remarkably American without losing any of
his alien allure? All I could find out from the jacket notes
was that Birnbaum was born in Washington, D.C., in 1957,
grew up in Japan, and lived at various times in Los Angeles,
Tokyo, London, and Barcelona.

Then *The Wind-Up Bird Chronicle* came out. This may
still be Murakami's best-known novel in America; it was his
first crossover book, the one that signaled his emergence from
the ghetto of Kodansha to the more exclusive precincts of
Knopf. I started the first chapter as soon as the book was
available, but right away I sensed that something was wrong.
Turning to the front of the book, I noticed the name of a
new translator: Jay Rubin. What had happened to my dear
Birnbaum? I called Kodansha, Knopf, the Society of Translators—no answer. Nobody knew anything about the missing
Birnbaum. He had apparently completed the transformation
required of The Ideal Translator and become a figment, a
ghost, an invisible man.

But then I remembered some additional evidence of his
corporeality, or at least of his presence as a translator. Before
publishing his novel with Knopf, Murakami had given that
same publisher a collection of short stories called *The Elephant
Vanishes*, and the first story in the book consisted of the
opening section of *The Wind-Up Bird Chronicle*. I checked
my copy of the book, and yes, my memory had not de-
ceived me—that story, that beginning, had been translated
by Alfred Birnbaum. So the two translators of Murakami,
the two alternate realities, existed side by side.

Here, submitted as Exhibit A, are the opening sentences
of the Rubin translation:

When the phone rang I was in the kitchen, boiling a potful
of spaghetti and whistling along with an FM broadcast of
the overture to Rossini's *The Thieving Magpie*, which has to
be the perfect music for cooking pasta.

I wanted to ignore the phone, not only because the spaghetti was nearly done, but because Claudio Abbado was
bringing the London Symphony to its musical climax.

Not bad, eh? Perfectly good English sentences presented by a
reasonably interesting narrator. But now listen to Exhibit B:

I'm in the kitchen cooking spaghetti when the woman calls.
Another moment until the spaghetti is done; there I am,
whistling the prelude to Rossini's *La Gazza Ladra* along
with the FM radio. Perfect spaghetti-cooking music.

I hear the telephone ring but tell myself, Ignore it. Let
the spaghetti finish cooking. It's almost done, and besides,
Claudio Abbado and the London Symphony Orchestra are
coming to a crescendo.

And there he is, my Birnbaum—or rather, my voice-in-
the-ear version of Murakami, my Birnbaum-inflected Japanese narrator, my unemployed cosmopolitan wastrel who
loves jazzy rhythms and thinks of his life in the present tense.
Even the small details (the Italian rendering of the Rossini
title, the use of the term "crescendo" rather than "musical
climax") seem to me crucial to the smart but strangely innocent voice. In this translation, the logic of cause-and-effect
English sentence structure has been jettisoned in favor of
some other mode, and it is that mode—the intrusion of the
surprising and the foreign and the unknowable into the mundane regime—which marks the world of a Haruki Murakami
novel.

I adapted, eventually, to Jay Rubin's perfectly good translations, and even to the slightly more whimsical voice of Philip Gabriel, who did the English for some of Murakami's more recent novels. (Both Rubin and Gabriel worked on the gigantic *1Q84*, and I have to admit I couldn't tell the difference between their sections.) But all along, the Birnbaum passion simmered. So you can imagine how the flame leapt up when I finished the Rubin translation of *Norwegian Wood*— Murakami's first huge bestseller in Japan, published there in 1987, but not brought out in America until 2000—and read a reference in the Translator's Note to "Alfred Birnbaum's earlier translation of *Norwegian Wood*, which was produced for distribution in Japan . . . to enable students to enjoy their favorite author as they struggled with the mysteries of English." We should *not*, the note enjoined us, try to obtain this bootleg version, for "the present edition is the first English translation that Murakami has authorized for publication outside Japan."

Naturally I sought out the bootleg version immediately. Thanks to the internet, such things are readily available, if at a shocking price: the two little paperbacks of the Kodansha English Library edition cost me more than a hundred dollars. Not surprisingly, I found that the Birnbaum version *was* better, in exactly the way his opening sentences of *The Wind-Up Bird Chronicle* were better. But I have yet to read the whole of the Alfred Birnbaum *Norwegian Wood*. I am saving them for a rainy day, those two cunningly miniaturized volumes, a red one and a green one, each encircled with a band of metallic paper covered in Japanese writing. They're like a souvenir brought back from a country I've never visited—a strange hard-boiled wonderland of wild sheep and vanished elephants, a place that never existed except in the imaginary terrain inhabited jointly if briefly by Haruki Murakami and Alfred Birnbaum.

If you can lose an author through a change in translator, you can also gain one in the same way. I found this out with Dostoyevsky, who by now has benefited from more than a century of good translators, beginning with the remarkable Constance Garnett and going on to include David Magarshack, Sidney Monas, David McDuff, Andrew MacAndrew, and many others. Dostoyevsky's latest English incarnation is the work of Richard Pevear and Larissa Volokhonsky. To date these two have translated *The Brothers Karamazov*, *Crime and Punishment*, *The Idiot*, *Demons* (their name for *The Possessed*), *The Adolescent* (elsewhere called *A Raw Youth*), and a number of the shorter novels, such as *Notes from Underground*, *The Double*, and *The Gambler*. What I found when I read their *Demons*, my earliest encounter with one of their translations, was that I consciously perceived, for the very first time, that strange narrator who is both there and not there, who comes in when the author needs him and quietly disappears when he doesn't. Pevear and Volokhonsky have done something with Dostoyevsky's language—I don't know exactly what or how—so that you can actually *hear* that ingratiating, whiny, gossipy, unreliable, all-seeing fellow who conveys the story to you.

Once you have had your ears opened to this, you can go back to the Magarshack or the Garnett and hear it in them as well. The narrator, it turns out, was there all along, but it took these new translators to make me aware of him. So in giving us their own insightful version of this great Russian novelist, Pevear and Volokhonsky have magically enriched all the previous versions. Perhaps it takes a writer as large and multi-voiced as Dostoyevsky to make room for all these translators at once. Or perhaps it takes someone who has been dead for over a hundred years, so that several generations of interpreters are required to convey him to us. But either way, it gives me hope. As long as a literary work is there in its original language, however inaccessible to me, there remains the possibility that it will eventually be given a new voice with which to speak its old lines. The new version will not quite duplicate the original—nothing can ever do that—but it will at least get me a step closer to my golden prison's exit.

All translation work is underpaid and underpraised, but there is one kind of translation which, in my experience, operates almost completely beneath the radar, and that is the translation of mystery novels. Thanks to all this skillful drudgery, I have spent many of my most pleasurable and certainly my most addictive reading hours in an imaginary Scandinavia. Though I've never been to Stockholm, Oslo, or Copenhagen, I know the street names in these cities almost as well as European teenagers of the mid-twentieth century knew the landmarks of New York and Los Angeles. Their tour guides were American movies. Mine were the thrillers and mysteries of Per Wahlöö and Maj Sjöwall, Henning Mankell, Arne Dahl, Jo Nesbø, and a long list of other Scandinavian authors, all of whose craftsmanlike works were brought to me by equally craftsmanlike—that is to say, nearly invisible—translators. Without looking them up, I cannot tell you the translators' names; from a readerly point of view, their identities have merged completely with those of their respective authors.

What is it about Scandinavian mysteries that makes them, on average, so much better than anyone else's? I'm not saying Americans can't write good thrillers: Ross Macdonald's Lew Archer series would come near the top of any aficionado's list, as would Patricia Highsmith's Ripley books. But these psychological, individualistic portraits of twisted motivation represent only a sliver of what the genre can do. In the right hands, the mystery novel becomes not only a thrilling cat-and-mouse game between a clever murderer and a persistent detective, but also a commentary on the wider society that spawns, polices, and punishes murder. It is this aspect, the wider, social view, at which the Scandinavians excel.

Perhaps one can attribute this in part to the small size of these far northern countries, their relatively homogenous populations, their stable cultural traditions—a setting, in short, in which murders, and especially serial murders, stand out starkly and beg for analysis. Or maybe this wider focus is connected to the firmly if mildly socialist perspective of even the most conservative Scandinavian governments, a view in which individual behavior contributes to or detracts from the public welfare. Possibly the dark, cold, long winters also have a role: with those extreme alternations between everlasting night and midnight sun, the Swedes, Danes, and Norwegians may be more likely than the rest of us to reflect on the role of environment in shaping character. The citizens of these countries also seem unusually alert to their own national pasts (unlike Americans, say, for whom the mid-twentieth century is already History), and this in turn makes them more likely to seek cause and effect in these collective historical influences. In any event, what all these factors add up to is a worldview that places the criminal at the center of a social web. This is not necessarily what makes Scandinavian mysteries addictive—*that* can probably be attributed to the more usual thriller qualities of suspense and surprise—but it accounts for at least part of what makes them satisfying, in that you reach the end of each novel with a sense of fulfillment rather than letdown.

The greatest of all Scandinavian mysteries are undoubtedly the Martin Beck series, ten sequential volumes written in the late 1960s and early 1970s by the Swedish husband-

and-wife team Maj Sjöwall and Per Wahlöö, who sought to convey a changing Swedish society through the crimes investigated by Detective Beck and his band of policemen. Closer to our own time, the worthiest inheritors of the Sjöwall-Wahlöö mantle that I've been able to find are Henning Mankell's Kurt Wallander novels. I should pause here, though, to admit (for once) that my "undoubtedly" is not universally agreed to. Louise Glück—who in her own way is as much of a mystery addict as I am—believes that the Kurt Wallander books are even greater than the Martin Beck series. She has read and reread each volume many times, and at least one of her own poetry collections, *Averno,* is infused throughout with images that she privately but very consciously borrowed from the Wallander novels. Where I find Mankell's sentences serviceable, she finds them compelling and evocative. She is so adamant in her devotion, and so effective in her expression of it, that she has almost begun to shake my own conviction about the superiority of the Martin Becks.

I began reading the Kurt Wallander novels in the final years of the twentieth century, when they first started appearing in English, and I have reread most of them at least once since then. The first one, *Faceless Killers,* was published in Swedish in 1991, and after that they came out on a nearly annual basis, with each book set about a year earlier than its date of publication. What this topicality meant was that Mankell was often riding the wave of history before it had even had time to break on our shores. The 1992 *Dogs of Riga,* for instance, anticipated the disarray into which the Soviet Union and its satellite states would soon fall; the 1993 *White Lioness* was even more prescient about the dying gasps of apartheid in South Africa. Part of the reason for reading Mankell obviously lies in his penetrating social and political vision. He occupies a larger world than ours (than mine, anyway: he spends part of each year in Sweden and the rest directing a theater company in Mozambique), and he is able to make a great deal of what he observes in that world. But to rest the praise for the Kurt Wallander series entirely on this largeness would be to ignore what is perhaps best about the books: their rueful, tender attention to detail.

The books are compulsively readable, but that is not because they pack one wallop after another. On the contrary, part of what makes them so easy to sink into is the relative leisureliness of their pace. We spend a lot of time with Kurt Wallander doing his laundry, or rather, forgetting to do his laundry and having to sign up once again for a slot in his apartment building's laundry room. We watch him make shopping lists, stop for hamburgers at fast-food restaurants, take his old Peugeot in for repairs or replacement, go to the doctor, visit his elderly father, call his daughter on the phone, and check the thermometer outside his kitchen window. There is a lot of reference to the weather in these books, and most of it is not case-related: it is instead a central element in the small-town Swedish world which becomes, for the duration, our world. We learn the street names of Ystad (the town in the Skåne region where Wallander lives and works), and we learn that it is possible to walk from Wallander's apartment on Mariagatan to a downtown restaurant, or from the police station to the local hospital. Probably no detective in literature—and certainly no other overweight detective—has done more casual walking than Wallander. I guess the others are all in too much of a hurry, or else they live in places where you can easily catch a cab or the subway. Wallander is not slow, but he's methodical. When he's on a case, he'll often work halfway through the night and still show up at the station by seven the next morning. (The books are very precise about reporting the time of day and the day of the week.)

There are occasional moments of sudden tension, shoot-outs and car chases and the like, but mainly what we do in these books is watch Wallander think.

The detective form has always been well suited to showing us thought processes—look at Sherlock Holmes and his carefully explained deductions—but Henning Mankell goes a step further. Thought, in Mankell's hands, is not entirely logical or rational, though it can be both; it is also the hunch, the instinct, the unconscious realization. Sometimes we spend two or three pages just sitting with Wallander while he reads through the case file once again. Sometimes we watch as he looks at photographs, or stands quietly in a victim's apartment, hoping to be able to spot the one thing that's not quite right. Fully half of Wallander's time seems to be spent waiting for these elusive thoughts to rise to the surface. The solution, or part of it, floats at the corner of his mind, just out of reach, and if he turns to face it directly, it darts away. It is this motion, of the mind's attempt at retrieval, that is the most characteristic and alluring action in the Wallander mysteries. And it is perhaps this ongoing process of *watching thought take place* which explains why we don't, at the end of a Wallander book, feel the usual letdown of the mystery novel. The arrival at the solution is not all that matters; a great deal of the interest, and the pleasure, comes from how we got there. This is why the books can be compelling even on a second or third reading: even if you think you have picked them up again to skim for the plot, you will find yourself willy-nilly relaxing into that luxurious, detail-studded pace.

All ten Inspector Wallander books have by now been translated into English, including a belated volume of stories, long available only in German and Swedish, called *The Pyramid: The First Wallander Cases*. The translations—from three different translators: Laurie Thompson, Ebba Segerberg, and Steven T. Murray—are unobtrusive, and that is a great virtue. In fact, I am tempted to say, though of course I don't know them in Swedish, that the writing in the Wallander books is itself unobtrusive. The sentences of the Wallander books (with all due respect to Louise Glück) do not beg to be read aloud as poetry. That is not their strength. Like Wallander himself, they are serviceable, methodical, decent, and often transparent, though capable of hiding information at times. They are the perfect medium in which to transmit thought, which can be fragmentary and inchoate as well as solid and complete. Their unobtrusiveness is, in this respect, their most valuable quality, for it enables us to feel that the thoughts are coming to us direct.

You can read the Wallander books in any order you choose, which is what I did the first time around. As mysteries they are entirely self-contained, and the personal material is recapitulated often enough for outsiders to catch up. Even on your first exposure to a Wallander novel, you will soon learn the names of Wallander's regular colleagues, the status of his relationship with his longtime Latvian girlfriend, the nature of the current job held by his daughter, Linda, and the fact that his elderly father, a painter, has spent a lifetime executing a series of nearly identical sunset landscapes, some with a grouse and some without.

But if you start with *Faceless Killers* and work your way chronologically forward to the end of the series, you will get something else besides. As with the Martin Beck mysteries, you will be treated to the unfolding of a life over time. In the first novel, Wallander is forty-two. He has been separated from his wife for only a few months, his daughter is barely speaking to him, and he is just beginning to worry about his bad eating habits, his loneliness, his disillusion with police work, and the other concerns that will increasingly plague him over the long term. By the time we get to *Firewall*, it is 1997 and Wallander is fifty years old. His old father has died, but not before taking an important final trip to Rome with him. Wallander himself is by now suffering from diabetes but still can't seem to control what he eats. Though he is proud of his professional achievements, he is more than ever aware of his shortcomings and feels himself slipping behind: computers, for instance, have taken over the police station, and Wallander is the only one who still doesn't know how to use them. The crimes he has to deal with have become more impersonal, more violent, and more widespread. In the course of the seven years and nine books, one colleague, a reliable if somewhat dull and underappreciated police officer, has been murdered; another, who started out as a promising, fresh-faced cadet, has turned out to be an ambitious backstabber. So Wallander, always a bit of a loner, now has fewer people than ever to confide in. On the other hand, he has grown closer to the one female detective in his squad, and his daughter, now on cordial terms with him, is talking about joining the police herself. So there is, if not hope, at any rate a future.

Henning Mankell, having created this paragon of quotidian survival, eventually became anxious to distance himself from Kurt Wallander. "If we met, we'd never get on," he told an interviewer from *The Guardian*, shortly after the English-language publication of *Firewall*. "I'd prefer to meet Sherlock Holmes. Wallander has a strange attitude to women. He is lazy in his personal life." But then he added, as if disturbed by it, "Women readers adore him. Perhaps they sense he is needy. What interests me is the way he is thinking. You can have six or seven pages when that's all he is doing." Perhaps that's what interests the women readers, too. Adoration, in any case, does not seem the appropriate word here. We have

enough literary figures who arouse our strong passions, the
kinds of characters who flame up with a brief intensity and
then die before their novels are over. Sometimes—maybe especially in these times—we just need someone who can endure.

But Mankell, unfortunately, has other plans for us. We
are not to be allowed to ask for Wallander again and again;
we are not to depend on him forever. The final book in the
series, *The Troubled Man*—which came out more than a decade after *Firewall*, a period during which Mankell obviously
tried unsuccessfully to ignore Wallander—is quite emphatic
about that. In the course of resolving this book's mystery,
Kurt begins to lose his memory and have serious blackouts.
At the very end of the novel, the narrator tells us, in an
uncharacteristically distant voice, that what we have witnessed are the early stages of Alzheimer's, a disease which
will eventually obliterate character (and, as it happens, *this*
character) entirely. This kind of authorial destructiveness, I
might point out, is the same pattern acted out by Arthur
Conan Doyle in relation to his detective, Sherlock Holmes.
In each case, the despairing writer realizes he has invented a
character who has grown larger than himself, an uncontrollable figure who clambers across the supine authorial body as
he makes his way into the arms of the demanding public.
And the writerly impulse at this point is always the same: to
eliminate the detective in order to make his return impossible.
I am sorry Mankell felt he had to end the series so vehemently.
It would have been better just to leave us hanging—unsatisfied,
perhaps, but also unpunished.

There is one other kind of "elsewhere" I want to glance at
before leaving this chapter, and that is the realm of science

fiction. Science fiction writers, it turns out, are also translators of a sort. They take the reality around them and exaggerate it, or imagine it, into something else, and in doing so they produce a tale that is often an allegory of their own times. This is, in a way, the opposite of the transparency that the mystery translator pulls off. The writing in a science fiction novel, though generally undistinguished as writing, points to itself as a symbolic code, a scrim between the reader and the "real" story that lies behind. Interpretation is a given: the science fiction story begs to be unraveled as social commentary or philosophical message, even as it also amuses us on its own grounds. So, although the form is billed as a kind of escapism, we cannot simply immerse ourselves in the science fiction novel. Instead, we need to be constantly withdrawing from it and considering it from the distance of our own lives.

Where other translators transport us geographically, to places we may never have visited but instead come to know largely or entirely through their works, science fiction writers move us through time. This is a place we *have* all visited, if we have lived any number of years. So the feeling of time travel, as rendered in a work of science fiction, can seem oddly circular to a reader inhabiting the multiple dimensions of the remembered past, the actual present, and the writer-prophesied future. And because of the peculiar way we read science fiction—with one foot in our own time and one in the imagined world's time, the better to perceive the inevitable allegory—we are more than usually aware of the traveling that is being required of us.

Let me give an example of what I mean, using a novel by Isaac Asimov that was published nearly sixty years ago.

We inhabit a world in which weekly newsmagazines, printed on paper in columns of type, are considered primitive and profoundly obsolescent; in which an entire bookshelf of bound volumes can be stored in a gadget the size of a finger-tip; in which a mechanical device that is only about four inches long and a fraction of an inch thick can record whatever we like, play it back to us through a tiny earpiece, and rest comfortably in a pocket when not in use; in which space flight has been invented but is rarely used by humans, who have lost interest in it after the initial decades of excitement; in which handheld or easily portable computers are a commonplace item; in which literature can hardly be distinguished from film in the public mind; and in which some members of society long fruitlessly for a past era when all such developments were unknown and almost inconceivable.

We *do*, in fact, live in such a world, but I mean something else. The sentences I've just written are intended to characterize the world of Asimov's *The End of Eternity*, a science-fiction novel which is set in the 482nd, 575th, and 111,394th centuries, and which first appeared in print in 1955.

For those of you who were not around then (and I barely was: I was three at the time), let me assure you that none of the present-day realities mentioned above was even a mote in a scientist's eye. In 1955—which was the year my family, having come north from Los Angeles to San Jose, moved permanently to Palo Alto—my father was working for IBM, where he helped invent the huge mainframe computer that would eventually become the great-great-great-grandfather of Macs and PCs alike. By 1966 or 1967, when I first began reading Isaac Asimov novels, a version of that mainframe had recently become available for use in the high-school computing classes of a few advanced communities, so that some of us in the Palo Alto school system were instructed in the laborious inscription of punch cards to be fed into the mechanical maw—a process so inhuman and alienating and difficult, so resolutely *digital* in its outlook, that I was determined never to have anything to do with computers again. This resolve disintegrated in about 1983, when I purchased my first "personal computer," a boxy Kaypro whose 74-kilobyte brain, laughably minute by today's standards, was nonetheless more powerful (or so the salesman told me) than the mainframe that flew a man to the moon in 1969. And this is not to speak of laptops, cellphones, flash drives, iPods, DVDs, e-readers, and all the other devices which only came into widespread use in the last two decades or so. Asimov thought all this would take many centuries; instead, it took less than a generation. And yet if he was wrong about the timing, he was fantastically right about not only the inventions themselves, but the effect they would have on society.

Part of the pleasure of reading old science fiction is precisely this: with the special powers vested in you by historical hindsight, you can compare the playfully visionary forecasts with what actually took place. This puts you somewhat in the position of Asimov's "Eternals," the characters in *The End of Eternity* who stand outside of time, observing and controlling the vast majority who still live within it. The Eternals, contrary to what their name suggests, do not live forever; they age and die just as normal people do. But they have such extensive powers of technical analysis that they are capable of predicting what will happen to any individual human or group of humans. And because they also have at their beck and call an easy form of time travel—consisting of "kettles" that whiz along preset pathways in the fourth dimension, taking them many centuries "upwhen" or "downwhen"—they can actually enter into history at specific points in time and repeatedly change it. These so-called Reality Changes might involve something as small as moving a container from one shelf to another, or as large as engineering the deaths of a dozen people in a crash. The aim is always to produce the

Maximum Desired Response (M.D.R.) with the Minimum Necessary Change (M.N.C.): to insure, in short, that the unpleasant or antisocial or generally disruptive event does not occur, and to keep mankind in a state of comfortable if slightly dull equilibrium.

Though technology is what makes this kind of reality control possible, only a human being is capable of finding exactly the right moment and method of change. "Mechanical computing would not do," Asimov's typically invisible, intangible narrator tells us. "The largest Computaplex ever built, manned by the cleverest and most experienced Senior Computer ever born, could do no better than to indicate the ranges in which the M.N.C. might be found. It was then the Technician, glancing over the data, who decided on an exact point in that range. A good Technician was rarely wrong. A top Technician was never wrong." And then, in the kind of portentous single-sentence paragraph in which science fiction delights, Asimov adds: "Harlan was never wrong."

Harlan is our hero, a man whose "homewhen," or time of origin, is the 95th century, but who as a teenager was lifted out of Time to become one of the Eternals. (The capitals, I hasten to note, are all Asimov's.) Like all Eternals, he can never go back to his own century—not only because the rules forbid it, but because if he went back he would, like Jimmy Stewart in *It's a Wonderful Life*, find everything horribly changed. He would learn that he had never had a home or a mother or an existence of any kind, because the ongoing series of Reality Changes (some, perhaps, implemented by himself) would have wiped him off the record. So instead he travels light, moving from one century to another, putting in the fix as needed, obeying his superiors, and only occasionally wondering why life is structured the way it is and whether Eternity really lasts forever.

I won't go any further into the plot of this novel. If you have never been a science fiction fan, I will long since have lost you anyway. But if you ever *were* a fan—as I was, quite obsessively, in my teens—you cannot do better than to return to the works of Isaac Asimov. Cheesy as the love story inevitably is, and inconsistent as some of the time-related logic turns out to be (why, for instance, does Harlan have to cancel an appointment in the 575th century in order to go to the 3,000th and see a man who is "free this afternoon," when normal logic tells us he could have gone and returned in a matter of minutes, or even seconds?), the essential storyline has a deeply compelling quality that is, at least to me, irresistible. As I approached the end of this novel, I found myself agitatedly turning pages in the way I always do in the last hundred pages of a Henry James novel. And, as in the James novel, the propulsive force was a desire to find out how things turn out for these deeply knowing but finally helpless characters, who are up against moral dilemmas they can't easily solve, and who are impeded in their attempted solutions by people who are often socially and economically more powerful than they are.

(In case you feel yourself preparing to get into an argument right about now, let me just say that I am *not* insisting Isaac Asimov is as good as Henry James. That would be absurd, just as it would be pointless and silly to assert that Henry James is a better writer than Isaac Asimov. Reading is not a ratings game, and to treat it as one is to diminish its pleasures and powers. Very little in the world can compare with the experience of reading, or even rereading, *The Golden Bowl*, but we cannot always be reading *The Golden Bowl*. Our moods and our tastes require other diversions, other satisfactions. The inveterate reader is not always looking for the Top Ten, the winnowed winners; on the contrary, she is likely to be seeking out precisely those kinds of immersive experiences that allow her to forget all about such invidious comparisons. And Isaac Asimov's novels, at their best, are good enough to accomplish this.)

The End of Eternity may be one of Asimov's better novels, but it follows the same essential pattern as all his others, as I discovered when I went back recently to reread Foundation's Edge and The Robots of Dawn. Like all obsessive writers, including Henry James, Isaac Asimov is the victim of a repetition compulsion, reproducing a single novel over and over again in all its myriad forms. His goes something like this: An individual with good powers of analysis and logic, as well as a great deal of modestly worn courage, confronts a gigantic system that is out to thwart him because he threatens, wittingly or unwittingly, to bring about its downfall. In the course of his efforts, he has to rely on other people without knowing for sure which ones are his friends or lovers and which his enemies or betrayers. He is good at crossing cultural boundaries and even interacting with other life forms (some of Asimov's most touching relationships are those between human and robot), but he retains a stubborn, almost curmudgeonly affection for the values and sensations of his own home place. Generally this place is Earth, and even when it is not, he and his entire culture have a kind of residual fondness—though also a civilized man's anti-primitive aversion, or an adult's anti-infantile one—toward that long-lost homeland, that long-gone birthplace of the human race.

One of the advantages of looking back on Asimov's work from the remove of several decades, not to mention the turn of a century, is that one can see how deeply enmeshed he was in the history of his own time. He was the child of Russian emigrants who left the Soviet Union for America in 1923, just three years after their son Isaac was born; and one can, if one chooses, view his whole science-fiction oeuvre as a re-capitulation of the Soviet experiment and the Cold War reaction to it. Yet these novels, although they wear their antitotalitarian garb as prominently as Orwell's ever did, are unlikely ever to be kidnapped by the right, for the simple reason that all the individualistic, novelty-mongering American virtues are countered in Asimov's work, and sometimes outweighed, by their opposites: that is, a belief in collective effort, a passion for the past, and an ineradicable pessimism about the prospects for human progress. For Asimov, super-civilization and technological achievement always go hand in hand with a general softening or weakening of the human spirit, and it is only by getting back to basics (or intuition, or felt sensation) that people can continue to move ahead. It is an essentially nostalgic view, and as such it is deeply Russian, however much Asimov may have felt himself to be a fully fledged citizen of his new country.

The note on the author attached to the 2010 reissue of *The End of Eternity* tells us that Isaac Asimov, in addition to writing vast quantities of science fiction, "taught biochemistry at Boston University School of Medicine and wrote detective stories and nonfiction books on Shakespeare, the Gilbert and Sulli-van operettas, biochemistry, and the environment. He died in 1992." But if we time-travel back to 1984, when the Ballan-tine paperback of *The Robots of Dawn* came out, we can pic-ture ourselves at a moment when the author himself was still alive. In the author's note to *that* book, we learn that "at the present time, he has published over 260 books, distributed through every major division of the Dewey system of library classification, and shows no signs of slowing up. He remains as youthful, as lively, and as lovable as ever, and grows more handsome with each year. You can be sure that this is so since he has written this little essay himself and his devotion to absolute objectivity is notorious." If you are one of those people who, like myself, are still committed to the primitive, cellulose-based habits of reading, you will find that the pages on which you read this are yellowed and flaking. But the voice they transmit, though it belongs to someone gone from this world for twenty years and more, is as strong and as vitally alive as ever.

SEVEN

INCONCLUSIONS

I am not fond of inconclusive endings, and I would not subject you to one if I didn't think it necessary. I believe as firmly as the next reader that the writer undertakes to deliver as promised, even if the promise is merely implied, and I too get annoyed when the delivery goes missing. Just the other night, for instance, I finished reading a mystery novel (not a very good one, so I won't bother to tell you its name) and was appalled by its author's cavalier attitude toward conclusions. We had reached the final page, with the serial killer safely tucked away in the police station, and one of the two detectives who had apprehended the murderer casually asked the other to hazard a guess about motive. What, she wondered, had caused the killer to commit his crimes in the first place—and why, having committed them, had he voluntarily sent in the obscure piece of evidence that in the end allowed him to be caught? "I doubt he knows the answer to that himself," the other cop replied, and that was all we ever learned on the subject. *This* was an ending? Clearly the author had just decided to pick up his check and go home early.

But in this case, I don't feel I am breaking even an implied promise. I never said we were going to get somewhere definite with this investigation. In fact, I recall suggesting that we were only going to go around in circles: glorified circles, perhaps, rising one upon the other in a pleasing spiral shape, but circles nonetheless. Like literature itself, this book does not make progress. It was never intended to. Yet it does hope to satisfy, and with that in mind, I will do my best to draw some tentative conclusions.

Certain patterns emerge only in retrospect. I said at the beginning that there were no essential subjects to be covered, no crucial facts to be conveyed, and yet I do seem to have zeroed in, in the course of the book, on many of the things that are central to my own motives as a reader. As I look back on this series of loosely linked chapters—this ring of circus elephants, you might say, each holding in its prehensile trunk the tail of the elephant in front of it—I notice that every chapter title answers, or at least attempts to answer, the question of why I read. This is a purely grammatical observation I'm making: each title fits syntactically into the blank space in the sentence "I read to find _____."

Yet the titles, though they are true enough, are inadequate to their task; or perhaps I mean that they are too much bigger than their task, too liable to encompass more than a single chapter's material. To give but one example: Consider that curiously intense yet impossible-to-pin-down relationship between the mirroring figures who occupy just about every work of literature I cite here, those twins or pairs separated by only the thinnest sliver of imaginary space. These pairs include not only the explicit "you" and "I" of a book or a poem, but also the novelist and his fictional protagonist, the essayist and her on-the-page self, the living reader and her dead author, even the literary character and his most salient, detachable characteristic. I have called this relationship "the space between" and located it in a chapter of that title, but it does not

reside neatly there. It floods over into every other subject, sur-
facing when I refer to Norman Mailer's approach to novelty,
or J. M. Coetzee's version of authority, or Dostoyevsky's brand
of intimacy; it persists even up to the last sentence of "Elsewhere," when I am talking about Isaac Asimov's beyond-
the-grave voice. And this flooding, this overflowing, is true
of every other subject I treat: character is everywhere, and so
is grandeur, and so is plot. So perhaps it is not a ring of separate elephants we have here, but just one big elephant wearing multiple disguises, one elephant standing in for the whole
idea of Elephant and trying to be them all. No wonder a
sense of incompletion is inevitable.

I still think it's possible, though, to make certain statements about literature that will hold true at least for a while,
and one of these statements is about the truth. I hope it is
clear to you by now how much this matters to me. If there is
anything I hate when I am reading a book, it is the sense that
I am being lied to. One can get this sense from fictional
works as well as nonfiction ones, and even with nonfiction it
is not entirely a matter of factual discrepancies. Lying can be
done through tone, through omission, through implication,
through context. Lies, as one twentieth-century writer notoriously said of another, can inhere even in words like "and"
and "the." I do not understand why anyone would *want* to lie
in a work of art—what is the point of giving up your most
valuable privilege, in the one place where you are freely allowed to tell the truth?—but I suppose it has something to do
with shame, or greed, or ambition, or some other extra-literary
motive. The compulsion to lie, which is personal, has nothing to do with making good art, which must on some level
be impersonal. Art needs to rest on truth, even if it does so
counterfactually. The satire of Swift's "A Modest Proposal,"
the allegory of Asimov's *The End of Eternity*, the impossible

longing expressed in Javier Marías's "When I Was Mortal" or Thom Gunn's "Death's Door"—these are all examples of counterfactual truth.

I am obviously parting company with Plato here, if he meant us to take literally his assertion about poets being liars. What I am *not* doing, though, is breaking ranks with those of my contemporaries who make a firm distinction between fact and fiction. Given the constant and purposeful blurring of these categories in the literary world these days, I should stress that I belong with those who still believe in the difference. These include not only newspaper editors, libel lawyers, and scientific watchdogs, but also many, if not most, writers and artists. We who struggle to establish the truth do not want the cavalier liars diluting our efforts and blackening the names of memoir, essay, and nonfiction. This is not to say that everyone needs to get everything right all the time. One is allowed to make factual errors through a combination of negligence and good intentions—even the blinkered law permits that. And not every document that contains factual errors is a fullblown lie. (Several of my favorite novels, and many of my favorite poems, fall into this category.) But an author who self-righteously proclaims that there is no real boundary between fact and fiction is not someone you should trust regarding either.

The subject of truth and untruth brings me, tangentially, to the question of the unreliable narrator in literature. It is not, I must admit, a mode I generally care for. I'm not talking about the narrator we can learn to hate—that is a different matter entirely, as Roberto Bolaño's *By Night in Chile* and Robert Browning's "My Last Duchess" both beautifully illustrate. The truly evil narrator who revels in his own wickedness can be a great pleasure, if sometimes an uncomfortable one. No, the fellow I'm objecting to is that foolish, pathetic guy who thinks he's telling us the whole story when we and the author are obviously meant, at least eventually, to see around him. This kind of irony is always too broad and at the same time too clubby to be satisfying. A sensitively intelligent author does not need to make himself, or us, feel brilliant at the expense of his duped character. Instead, he is likely to make us feel that we are all part of the same collusive process (as Henry James does, for instance), so that sometimes the characters seem to know more than we do, and sometimes we know more than they, but no one comes out firmly ahead. I hate that nudge in the ribs we always get at the end of an unreliable-narrator novel, which is why I so strongly prefer Ford Madox Ford's *Parade's End* to his more famous *The Good Soldier.* This is not the worst form of authorial lie, this misrepresentation of what the narrator understands or fails to understand, but it is indicative, to me, of a generally cavalier attitude toward the truth. I mind lying whether or not it applies to people who don't exist.

How do I know when the author of a fictional work is lying to me? Or rather, how do I *think* I know, since it is all finally a matter of feeling, and nothing could ever be proved in court? My response has to do, in part, with that notion of authority. An incompetent writer can fail to tell the truth even when he is telling us about something that really happened—for instance, when he was in second grade—and an authoritative writer can tell the truth even when he garbles some of the facts: witness *War and Peace.* Part of what I am listening for, in such cases, is a voice that convinces me from the start. It is a voice that comes into being on the very first page, as I am entering the world of the literary work, and it must inspire enough confidence in me, right there at the beginning, so that I am willing to depend on it to carry me through whatever we are about to experience together.

But the author's risk of losing me never disappears entirely. I could begin to mistrust her at any time, so she needs to keep assuring me—subtly, implicitly, without any strong-arming or defensiveness—that at each particular juncture we have not parted company or opinions. It is not an easy thing to pull off. I have found myself twenty pages into an excellent short story, only to discover, at that late date, that the writer had betrayed her main character. I have enjoyed hundreds of pages of a fine novel, only to learn that I and the characters were to be abandoned by the author at the very end. This happens even to brilliant writers. They are all capable of spoiling their own work.

Which is not to say that a flaw, even a very visible flaw, will necessarily bring the whole structure down. The poet Randall Jarrell once defined the novel as a prose narrative of some length that had something wrong with it, and while one might feel this is just a poet's way of taking aim at prose, it is not. Here's what Jarrell actually said, in explaining what happened whenever he loaned out one of his favorite novels, Christina Stead's *The Man Who Loved Children*: "I have lent it to many writers and more readers, and all of them thought it good and original, a book different from any other. They could see that there were things wrong with it—a novel is a prose narrative of some length that has something wrong with it—but they felt that, somehow, the things didn't matter." As the flaws in the books we love never do matter to us. (And I venture to say this can be as true of poetry as it is of prose— long poems, at any rate, and maybe even some short ones.)

For my own part, I cannot think of a book I have loved that is completely without imperfections of any kind. These shortcomings may be as glaring as the false, tacked-on, Tom-Sawyer-ish ending of *Huckleberry Finn*, and as pervasive as the sentimentality of Dickens's attitude toward young women, dying children, orphans, and poor people. The problem can involve a reliance on the patently unconvincing (as, for instance, in Sonia's religious redemption of Raskolnikov at the end of *Crime and Punishment*), or the simple omission of something essential (such as the chapter about Stavrogin's past misdeeds that was cut by the censors from *Demons*). I think I may even love these books not in spite of their flaws, but because of them. The imperfections offer the necessary space between—that gap which I need to leap over or that crevice into which I can insert myself to become an active part of the literary work's world.

The problems, in fact, are what seem to make the books I love not only inviting but discussable, with myself and with you. It is in worrying at the knot of a question, a question no doubt suggested to me by those little wrinkles and flaws, that I come to realize exactly what I think about a written work. A theater director once said to me, "When I'm reading a play that I'm about to put onstage, I read it over and over until I find the problem. It can be a little problem, such as how characters get from one room to another, or a big problem, such as why a certain character exists at all. But the problem is essential to my thinking. It's only when I find the problem that I begin to understand how I'm going to stage the play." I suppose the same is true of the books I write about.

This perhaps goes some way toward explaining why Dostoyevsky makes so many appearances here and Tolstoy so few. Dostoyevsky specialized in imperfections; at times one can feel he is *all* imperfections. But this very roughness allows one to cling to him—to get a foothold in the cliff face of his grandeur—whereas Tolstoy's marmoreal splendor can come across as smoothly slippery and coldly forbidding. Even Tolstoy isn't perfect, of course. But he tends to strike one as flawless from the distance created by memory.

The kinds of problems that invite one into a literary work do not remain the same over time. Dickens is as flawed as Dostoyevsky, and I love him just as much, yet he has barely deigned to make an appearance here. Is it that I have already thought about him too much? I don't think one can—and even if that were possible, Henry James would certainly fall into the same category. I think the reason is more likely to be that different books speak to you at different times in your life. I am sure Dickens and Tolstoy will come back to me eventually, but at the moment I find myself in greater need of James and Dostoyevsky. We may think we are choosing what books to read, but they choose us as well.

It is not just that some books have refused to put themselves forward for my consideration. Looking back on the ones I've discussed here, I can't help feeling that even those that presented themselves also insisted, to some extent, on remaining hidden. This is because no analysis, no description, can ever do full justice to a work of literature. Only the thing itself, rendered in full, can serve as a satisfying example; a snippet won't do. Yet even when I have reproduced a poem in full (as I did, for instance, with Gerard Manley Hopkins's "As king-fishers catch fire"), the attention paid to it doesn't seem adequate. Kay Ryan, whenever she reads her short poems before an audience, always reads each one twice, as if that's the least she can do to allow people to take it in. I would have reproduced the Hopkins poem twice if I thought I could get away with it. But then, I would have liked to reproduce all of *The Brothers Karamazov* as well, not to mention every other work I've mentioned. If I had done as I wished, I would have been left with no book of my own, just a library of other people's works. There are many times when I've been tempted to break off our conversation and say, "Don't listen to me. Just go read!"

It needn't be either/or, though. You can listen to me *and* go read. I suppose the great advantage of having a conversation of this sort is that it gives us a chance to linger on the smallest details. Pleasure reading is a hungry activity: it gnaws and gulps at its object, as if desirous of swallowing the whole thing in one sitting. But we need to slow down, and at times even come to a dead stop, if we are to savor all the dimensions of a literary work. I wouldn't love even the longest of these books as much as I do if they didn't sustain my interest at the level of the sentence. The novel, it turns out, consists equally of the small and the large, the sentence and the overarching structure. Both must contribute to the ultimate design; both must be sufficiently good—sufficiently great, even with their flaws—if one is to find the novel satisfying. And this can be as true of translated works, where the sentences are those of, say, Alfred Birnbaum or Margaret Jull Costa, as it is of the books written in English.

If anything, my interest in the sentence has grown over time. As a young person, I used to read more for plot and character: my eye would begin to drift toward the period if Dickens or James went on for too long. Now, though, I revel in the extra clauses and glide around the sinuous switchbacks with delight. I am better, now, at hearing the author's particular, intimate, humor-inflected voice expressed in his idiosyncratically constructed sentences, and it is that voice which remains my constant companion throughout the book. Like Thornton Wilder's Stage Manager or Conrad's linguistic mist, the companionable voice does not get between me and the characters; on the contrary, my awareness of its presence paradoxically helps me feel closer to them. Style, in this sense, does not function in opposition to content, but instead brings it forth and makes it real. In the novels I love, there is no battle between the individual sentence and the overall shape of the work, just as there is no conflict between authorial design and character self-determination. Each is the hand-maiden of the other, and serves its designated part.

I suppose this is even more obviously true of poetry. But I have just realized something, as I near the end of my self-imposed quest, where the pursuit of why I read has turned into a discovery of how I read. What I now understand is that I read poetry much as I read prose, and nonfiction in much the same way I read fiction. I read them all for meaning, for sound, for voice—but also for something I might call attentiveness to reality, or respect for the world outside oneself. The writer Harold Brodkey used to say, when he was alive, that literature consisted of one speaking voice plus one other genuinely existing thing. Or so I remember him saying. Perhaps I have simply amalgamated him to my own ideas, incorporated him into myself, as we do with our remembered dead. Perhaps he has amalgamated *me*, the way so many of my beloved writers, living and dead, strangers and familiars, have a habit of doing.

Sometimes it is hard to keep in mind that they were all living, once—even Milton; even Cervantes; even Sophocles. We shouldn't let time mummify them, as it tries to do. The best musicians, it seems to me, play Bach as if he had written the piece just yesterday, for them, and that is how one ought to read literature. But reading in this way entails maintaining at least two apparently contradictory beliefs. The first is that a good book exists as an independent entity, completely outside of time. The second is that every book is the specific creation of a particular person at a precise historical moment.

For many years I labored under the delusion that biography and history dragged good art down, forcing it into generic categories. Now I know that is not the case. Nothing can drag a good work of literature down, and any additional insights that help you get a fix on it are to be welcomed. If the new information doesn't help, it can be ignored with no harm done: the work itself is strong enough to withstand any such intrusions. With that in mind, I have occasionally brought in bits of biographical or historical information about some of the authors I discussed here. The function of such description was never to "explain" the literary works; explanation is neither required nor fully possible, when it comes to literature. If I offered a few biographical facts about the men and women who wrote these books, it was because I know such information interests us (as Wilkie Collins might have said) for the perfectly obvious reason that we are men and women ourselves.

Because every author was originally a human being, capable of making errors and sometimes capable of correcting them, there is nothing predestined about the way any work of literature turned out. From the perspective of hindsight—which is our own perspective, as readers—the greatest books, and even some of the less great, may appear to have a quality of inevitability. But that was never actually the case. They could have gone this way or that. Some of the greatest *did* go this way *and* that, and we still can't be sure which version we should be keeping. Think of Henry James, with his early and late editions, the latter entailing a massive, detailed rewriting of his own youthful style. Think of William Wordsworth, who did much the same thing, but more extensively and, many think, more damagingly, with his early and late poetry. And think of Shakespeare, with all those textual "cruxes"—those little crossroads, those moments of verbal discrepancy, at which numerous scholars are still parting ways.

Before I ever had anything to do with the theater, I

thought that the Shakespearean cruxes were entirely attributable to transcription errors. When Othello refers in some texts to a "base Indian" who threw away a pearl, and in others to a "base Judean," I figured that was just because the written *I* and the written *J* looked so much alike. But now, having watched rehearsals at which playwrights changed their words until the last minute (and even sometimes after that), I wonder. The mistake wasn't necessarily a mistake. It could have been that Shakespeare made both choices at different times: one pointing toward that exciting New World which had only recently been discovered, or else that exotic Eastern world after which the New World inhabitants were named; another toward the anti-Semitism that represented a different kind of prejudice—a prejudice Shakespeare had fully explored in an earlier play—rather than the one his black Othello suffered under. These by no means exhaust the possibilities. And *Othello* doesn't necessarily become a better play or a worse play with either choice: just very slightly different.

The question of "better" and "worse" hovers over this book, because in talking about why I read and what I read, I am making judgments at every turn. I do not now intend to shy away from these judgments. They are at the heart of my enterprise. I would just like to stress that they too, like the works they apply to, could have come out differently. It is impossible for any one person, or even a large collection of people, to make literary judgments that will last for all time, or even for a lifetime. Knowing this, I have determined to practice to the full my right to be wrong. This is why I have included so many odd genres—science fiction, mysteries, journalism, diaries—along with the usual varieties of traditional literature. This is why I have cited living authors and even writers I know as well as those long dead. I would like the act of judging to be full of risk and vitality; I would like it to be a real choice. I am not interested in creating a museum of approved works—or if

I am, it would be like the art collection Albert Barnes assembled in his house near Philadelphia, with remarkable Seurats and ageless Picassos hanging next to paintings by relative unknowns like Ernest Lawson and Charles Prendergast. For Barnes, they were all simply artists whose paintings he liked; the work of his contemporaries and near-contemporaries hadn't yet hardened into an established hierarchy. Not everything at the Barnes Foundation is equally good. But the collection as a whole is alive with Barnes's taste, and each room feels like a discovery.

I cannot, of course, hope to reproduce exactly this kind of experience in the pages of a book. At the Barnes Foundation, as at most museums, you can go through the rooms in any order you wish. With this book, on the other hand, you are tied to my whims. You must take each subject, each observation, in the order I choose to dole it out. (Though "choose" is a loaded word here, and probably not an accurate one: think about how compulsions work, and recollect those spirits who refuse to come when called.)

Literature is by its very nature linear, by which I mean not just that each line of poetry or prose leads to the next, but also that each chapter of a book is meant to follow the one before it. Ideas get carried through and plot gets carried out, in nonfiction as in fiction. Even a collection—of poems, of stories, of essays—has usually been arranged by the author in a precise sequence, so that you jump in midway at your own peril. That is as true of this book as of any other. Its plot, so to speak, is intended to be followed from beginning to end. I may talk about circles and spirals, but what I have really constructed, it would seem, is a line. This is not to say that there aren't digressions and anticipatory peeks and retrospective musings, but they are all meant to be encountered in the order in which they appear on the page.

Certain kinds of art—sculpture, painting, architecture,

and to some extent dance—free your glance to make its own choices, allowing it to roam as it wishes, focus on what it desires, and move at will from side to side or top to bottom. Even film, theater, and opera, though they are narrative art forms tied to the passage of time, leave some latitude for the eye: the plot may progress in a specific way, but the viewer's gaze can dart into corners, peek at what is going on in the background, and still remain rooted in the story. Literature is not like this. The written word moves relentlessly forward, and you are required to take in the sentences in the order in which they come. If you stop focusing for even an instant, you lose the train of thought and must go back. There is only one pathway, and you and the author must follow it together.

I have always found this to be one of the most salutary things about reading—that it forces me to submit to a pattern set by someone else. At any rate, that's the way it is when you read through a printed book, a series of pages whose sequence has been determined by their author. Who knows how long this will remain true? The prophecies about the future of the book are becoming increasingly dire, the various freedoms offered by the screen more alluring; linearity itself seems under threat. Yet I would be sorry to think that this benign form of limitation, essential to how and why I read, could ever completely disappear.

AFTERWORD: THE BOOK
AS PHYSICAL OBJECT

I have before me a cartoon from the May 7, 2012, issue of *The New Yorker*. In it, an older scholar, or monk, or scribe—a man wearing a long, double-pointed beard and a melon-shaped fur-trimmed hat—sits at a rough wooden table with a younger scribe who has his arms crossed triumphantly in front of him. The older man is examining something the younger one has clearly just brought him: a leather-bound, clasp-backed book whose pages he appears to be turning. "Nice," the older scribe is saying, "but as long as there are readers there will be scrolls."

I don't know if a young person would find this funny. I think it's dourly hilarious—not laugh-out-loud, fall-on-the-floor hilarious, but pointedly funny. The joke is at my expense. It spells the end of the world as I know it, and it catches my own tone and that of most of my friends exactly. We are confident that books, as books, will never be obsolete. However many people adopt the new technologies, we are convinced that those cherished objects with which we have filled our houses, and our lives, are here to stay. After all, how could other people, even those unimaginable people of the future, bear to live without them?

In my house—a house in which one book-filled room is

rather grandiosely called "the library," and in which various kinds of bound books have spilled over into four other rooms and the basement—fifty percent of the current inhabitants have already gone over to the dark side. My husband will no longer read a book printed on paper. An early adopter of all new technologies ("Inspector Gadget," we used to call him, after a cartoon character who was prominent during my son's childhood), my husband will only read what he can obtain on his Kindle or his iPad. If I have bought a new mystery and recommend it to him when I am done, he will not read the free book that is lying around our house. Instead, he will spend the additional $9.99 or $12.99 that it costs to get it digitally, and if it is not yet available in digital format, he will read something else in its place. Granted, he is always happy when I can recommend an old, out-of-copyright book that he can download at no cost, but that may be as much because he prefers nineteenth-century novels as because he is inherently thrifty. In any case, his affection for the paperless book is now matched by his explicit distaste for the heavy, dusty, un-self-illuminating bound version. He has become like one of those people in Gary Shteyngart's futuristic *Super Sad True Love Story*—people who think that actual books smell bad.

I, on the other hand, think they smell wonderful. Sometimes, when I have ordered an old book on the internet and it finally arrives in the mail, and after I have thrown away the packaging and poured myself a drink and sat down in my favorite chair, I open the cover and sniff the pages before I even start to read. I always think the smell of that paper goes with its feel, the tangible sensation of a thick, textured, easily turnable page on which the embedded black print *looks* as if it could be felt with a fingertip, even when it can't.

Okay, so I'm a fetishist. But I am not the kind of fetishist who routinely haunts antiquarian bookstores and spends hundreds or even thousands of dollars on first editions and other hard-to-get volumes. I don't care *that* much about the book as physical object, and in fact I'm somewhat opposed to its being valued excessively as a form of concrete art. One of the great things about books, I've always thought, is that they are mass-produced, so there isn't any such thing as the "original" one. The writer, unlike the painter or sculptor, can both keep his work and give it away, and my copy will be just as good as his, or yours. I like the egalitarian aspect of the printed book as work of art.

The digital book is also egalitarian, in its way, but as a work of art it lacks solidity. I'm not just talking about a printed book's heft or weight (which, I'll admit, can also be a disadvantage, to weak wrists or weary packers), but, more important, the way its print stays put on the page. When you read a digital book, the words can change size and reflow at the touch of a button. Page numbering, left-and-right layout, space breaks, type design—all this means nothing on an electronic reader, or means only something temporary, something to be manipulated by the Reader of the reader. Length and placement become infinitely malleable. A Victorian novel that is 875 pages long on my iPad becomes 2,933 pages on my iPhone; if I enlarge the type one size, those numbers become 1,030 and 3,647, respectively. If I then change the font from, say, Palatino to Cochin, the corresponding numbers go up again, to 1,284 and 3,995 (plus the whole reading experience may alter, either slightly or hugely, depending on what kinds of prior associations I have with those different typefaces).

What this means, in practice, is that someone who remembers specific passages in the spatial way I do—as in "I think it was on the left-hand side of the page, not more than two or three pages before a chapter break"—becomes lost in the amorphous, ever-varying sea of the digital page. Oh, sure, I can perform a word or phrase search using that little Sherlock Holmes–like magnifying glass, and eventually it will probably take me to my desired passage. This is immensely useful if you are away from home. But it feels like cheating to me; or rather, what it actually feels is *external*, as if something else (not I, not the Reader herself) is doing the remembering. So the process is not, for me, the same as leafing through the book I take off my own shelves, the exact book in which I first read that passage and through which it imprinted itself on me. That, I suppose, is the main reason why *this* entire book had to be written at home, in the place where almost all my books dwell, and not in the various other locations where I spend, hourly or seasonally, a good bit of time.

I do read, though, on both my iPad and my iPhone. Most of the mysteries I read these days are purchased in digital form, if they are available that way. When you want a mystery, especially a sequel to a mystery, you generally want it *right now*, and the e-book versions, with their near-instantaneous materialization on your tablet or e-reader, are designed to supply this kind of gratification. There is also something about the swish of a finger on a glassy surface, the sudden flip of the visual screen, that seems the perfect way of turning the page on a page-turner. One zooms through the book, mentally and actually. It is annoying that you can't then lend out or give away these newly finished mysteries, as I am in the habit of doing with my bound books, but I assume this is a technical glitch that will someday be resolved. For the moment, it is a difficulty that is more than made up for by the ease of acquiring and carrying around these often disposable novels. Recently I filled a whole ten-day period of foreign travel with the three collected volumes of Michael Connelly's excellent Harry Bosch mysteries, stored up on my iPad and waiting for me every time I had a spare moment to read. I like Harry Bosch just fine, but I don't plan on reading these novels again anytime soon, so it was with no compunction that I edited them off my screen once I was done.

I am also a great fan of Project Gutenberg and all its copyright-free nineteenth-century novels. If you wanted to read a bunch of thrillers but didn't feel like paying for Michael Connelly, you could just download thirty or forty Wilkie Collins mysteries. Gutenberg books tend to be slightly typo-addled, and there are occasional format problems at chapter and section breaks, but these are minor quibbles when the price and availability are so right. Writers I have spent a fortune acquiring in obscure hardcover editions—William Dean Howells, for instance, who for a long time was barely reprinted anywhere—can now be readily obtained at no cost whatsoever. And the books are eminently readable in this form. Surprisingly, I find that even Henry James works well in his digital manifestation. The last time I read *The Wings of the Dove*, it was mainly on my iPhone, as I commuted back and forth by subway or sat in a café. I don't recommend this for first-time readers of James: you might have a hard time keeping track of the sentence, much less the whole plot, on the phone's small screen. But if you already have an overall sense of where the novel is going, this is not a bad way to reconnect with its detailed pleasures.

In fact, the Victorian novel I mentioned a few paragraphs back, the one that grows from 875 to 2,933 pages when it moves from tablet to phone, is James's *The Tragic Muse*. I downloaded it from Gutenberg to both devices as I was preparing to read it again. The opening pages, though, gave no indication about whether this was the early version, which James wrote when he was in his forties, or the late-style rewrite, which he produced for the definitive New York Edition twenty years later. Though I like both versions well enough, not knowing which one I was reading gave me slight qualms. So I went to my own shelves and plucked off my Penguin Modern Classics paperback, which contained a helpful "Note on the Text." The three-paragraph note briefly explained the history of the rewrite, gave two small examples of its effects on this novel's style, and then announced: "Either text was equally available for this edition; after comparing them, the publishers have deliberately chosen that of the first edition (Macmillan 1890) on grounds of taste." On grounds of taste! When was the last time you read that in an unsigned scholarly note? I was so moved and persuaded by this commendable audacity that I instantly plunged into the Penguin, leaving my digital downloads untouched.

Digital editions are certainly not the only ones to suffer from editorial shortcomings. That can happen in bound books, too. Sometimes the omissions are all too purposeful, resulting from publishing-house economics which dictate that a multi-volume work is too expensive to print and that only a single-volume abridged edition will do. This is a problem that digitalization, with its elimination of paper, ink, and bindings— with its elimination, in a way, of the whole idea of length— would seem perfectly designed to solve. Unfortunately, you can't yet count on getting everything you want digitally, and I often feel that the choice about what to put online has been made with extreme arbitrariness. Why, for instance, can I download all the volumes of Ulysses S. Grant's memoirs and none of those by a much better writer, Alexander Herzen?

The Herzen autobiography, *My Past and Thoughts*, offered the occasion for one of my more extreme encounters with both the dangers and the rewards of seeking out a print edition. I can no longer remember how I first heard about the book—as a throwaway reference, I think, in a review on some other topic entirely, but such an interesting reference that I felt obliged to follow it up. I checked Project Gutenberg first: no

Herzen. Then, because there are no actual bookstores in my vicinity anymore (the last two, Cody's and Black Oak Books, disappeared about a decade ago), I resorted to the various sites that sell printed books via the internet. The only version of *My Past and Thoughts* that clearly fell within my budget was a paperback edition published by the University of California Press and edited by Dwight Macdonald. Fine, I thought: nice left-wing credentials, excellent scholarly reputation, no problem. So I ordered the paperback.

When it arrived, though, it turned out to be an abridged edition. Not knowing Herzen yet, I thought perhaps I could live with this. After all, a nine-hundred-page abridgement is still a big book. But I got a bad feeling about the editorial process when I read in Macdonald's preface that he had "regretfully" been forced to cut a long section from Volume Two called "A Family Drama." This was Herzen's own title for his agonized, self-examining, often frenzied account of an affair between his much-loved wife (she is actually one of the two intimates to whom he at times addresses the memoirs) and a close friend of his. I would not have thought this was the kind of thing that any editor in his right mind would cut for space-saving reasons. Still, I persisted with the Macdonald edition. And then, as I was closing in on the end of a youthful section called "Prison and Exile," I came across the following footnote:

> At this point Herzen begins the story of his wife, Natalie—his first cousin and, like him, the illegitimate child of a wealthy aristocrat: her solitary and unhappy childhood, their courtship and early married life. It takes up the last hundred pages of the first volume. They are omitted here—as are the last one hundred and seventy pages of the second volume, about their tragic later married life ("A Family Drama")—for reasons of theme and space as explained in the Preface. (D.M.)

At that point I threw the book on the floor. Really, I did. Then I picked it up and mailed it to my son (who is intensely interested in politics and history, and wouldn't mind as much as I did about the missing marital story), and got back online to search for the complete version.

I had learned enough from Dwight Macdonald's preface to know that the edition I wanted was the four-volume set published in 1968 by Chatto & Windus in England and Alfred A. Knopf in America. Based on Constance Garnett's original six-volume translation, this edition had been updated by Humphrey Higgens, who added a number of useful footnotes from various authoritative Russian editions as well as new Herzen material he'd dug up on his own. Most of the copies for sale on the internet were either incomplete ("Vol. 1 only") or ridiculously expensive. At last, however, I found what seemed to be the whole thing, offered by the Friends of Webster Groves Public Library for the very reasonable price of fifty dollars. I clicked on that one, inserting a long comment about which edition I was seeking and asking that the sale not go through until this had been verified. Since the order was placed on the Sunday of Memorial Day weekend, I assumed I wouldn't hear anything more until business reopened on Tuesday.

But that Monday, on the holiday itself, I got a response from someone named Ann. Thus began a brief but satisfying epistolary love affair between me and the Friends of Webster Groves Public Library. (I still have no idea where Webster Groves is. It sounds like something Thornton Wilder would have made up, and I prefer to keep it that way.) In that first note, Ann informed me that she thought the one they had was the four-volume edition, but she couldn't be sure until she checked it on Tuesday. I thanked her and wished her a happy Memorial Day. A few hours later, still on the holiday, I got another email:

Hi, Wendy. I was able to get to our book storage area and did find the 4 volume set of Herzen's My Past and Thoughts translated by Constance Garnett with revisions by H. Higgens. This is exactly as you described. It appears no one used these books, they are in excellent condition. I did notice the previous owner wrote her name on the inside front page. The cardboard case that comes with this set does have a tear down one side and it looks like one edge was hit against something and it has an indentation in the corner. The books are not affected. I brought this set home with me and can mail these to you tomorrow after I hear from you. Happy Memorial Day to you too. Ann Friends of Webster Groves Public Library.

Some of the pleasure I got from reading this book—which I did in full immediately after it arrived, and then again, in sections, over the years since—came from the warmth of that transaction. As I told Ann, I really *like* to own books that have the previous owner's signature in them, much as I enjoy living in a Victorian house, where the habits and tastes of its earlier residents are still discernible in places. And the edition itself was even lovelier than I had expected: the margins were generously wide, the pages were the beautiful thick kind, and the otherwise identical dust jackets were printed in four different colors. The volumes looked—and still look—marvelously substantial, sitting there in their yellow slipcase on my bookshelf, with the four black Borzois bounding across their spines. They could almost make one believe that books will last forever.

I lived for that whole summer with Herzen; he was my constant companion, even when I was not reading him. If I was out to dinner with friends, I would find myself thinking, "Who *are* these people? I want to be back with my *real* friends, Herzen and Natalie. I want to know what happens to them next." This is a little sick, but any avid reader will recognize the symptoms. One of my closest friends excused herself early from a dinner at my house by saying she had to get home to read *The Maias*, and I know exactly how she felt. For those of us in the midst of a good book, the characters' fates hang in the balance *now*. It matters to us not one whit that they were already fixed on the page a hundred years ago.

A digital-book proponent might point out that my Herzen experience would have been a lot more flexible and relaxed if I had managed to acquire the book on my iPad. I would not have been restricted to those moments when I happened to be seated in my well-lit, comfortable chair at home. The entire four volumes would have been lightweight, portable, and easy to read in out-of-the-way places such as subways, airplanes, cafés, or the living rooms of my friends' houses. I could even have read it in bed, without the assistance of a reading light and without straining my wrists or spreading dust on the bedsheets. While I read, I could have used earphones to listen to any background music I chose. And besides all this, I would have been able to interrupt my reading at any time to check email, or look at headline news, or do whatever else I might need to do at any hour of the day or night. The book and my regular life could have been completely integrated.

But that, you see, would be a disadvantage as well as an advantage. All the pluses of portability and multifunctionality are, to a certain kind of reader, simply undesirable distractions. Alexander Herzen resided, for me, in a specific place that summer, and whenever I retreated to that place, I was alone with him. This (in addition to his great writing style, his keen mind, and his remarkable material) is what made the experience of reading him so intimate, so immersive. I sat for hours doing nothing but reading. I didn't care about what was in my email inbox. I didn't care about breaking news.

I am not going to natter on here about the distractability

of the high-tech generation and the youthful inability to focus. That is not my point. We are all distractable. And reading has its own kind of distraction already built into it, as I learned (or was reminded) when I went to buy my first iPad.

I was having the new device set up for me at the store, which took more than an hour of intensive consultation. About halfway through this process, the smart young Apple-woman who was helping me with the setup wondered what I might want to do with the iPad besides the obvious functions of checking email and surfing the web. Read newspapers and magazines, I suggested. Write short things when I'm away from my computer. Listen to all the music I have stored up on my iPod. And read books. "In fact," I added enthusiastically, "I guess now I can listen to my music and read a digital book at the same time, when I'm on a long airplane flight or something."

She nodded in a friendly way, and then told me that she actually preferred to use her own iPad to listen to audio books. "It's easier for me to concentrate if I'm listening," she explained. "When I read with my eyes, sometimes I find that my mind drifts and I have to reread the same sentence over again to find out what it means."

I looked at her for a second in silence. "That's how reading works," I said.

In my more broad-minded moments, I am willing to acknowledge that there is no inherent difference between reading from a printed page and reading from an electronic device. It just depends on what you are used to. Those of us who have grown up reading bound books will miss them if they disappear, not because printed books are objectively preferable, but because we will feel deprived of something we care about. Daniel Kahneman, in his book *Thinking, Fast and Slow*, writes intelligently about the difference between gaining something and losing something. It turns out that people are, as he puts it, "loss averse"—that is, we are more likely to make a decision that allows us to keep something we already have than to gamble on something that, in economic terms, is equally valuable. Before Kahneman demonstrated this through a variety of psychological experiments, economists had pretty much assumed that all such choices were made on purely rational grounds, dollar for dollar, benefit for benefit. But Kahneman showed that whereas Econs (his term for the mythical beings who populate economic theory) would always choose according to the exact mathematical odds, Humans valued what they already possessed over what might be gained, and therefore slanted their risk-taking decisions toward retention rather than acquisition. So for me, for any of us, to want to keep our physical books on our physical bookshelves is not necessarily a sign that we are Luddites. It just means that we are Humans rather than Econs.

Robert Pinsky has written a poem called "Book" that celebrates, in part, this old-fashioned attachment to the physical object. It was originally composed as part of a series called *First Things to Hand*, a collection of poems about the various objects that the poet could reach out and touch with one hand while he was sitting at his desk. From the poem's opening lines, the tactility of the actual book—its feel, its physical presence, its riffled pages that "brush my fingertips with their edges"—is primary. But this first sensation gradually modulates in the course of the poem into something else, something more abstract and metaphorical, something more to do with spirit or essence. So, about halfway through, the poet alludes to the "reader's dread of finishing a book, that loss of a world," along with an opposite dread, the fear of becoming "Hostage to a new world, to some spirit or spirits unknown." It is a vision of reading which reminds us that even the thing to hand, beloved as it may be, is secondary to the voice it stands in for, that absent speaker who might once have declaimed his lines aloud but who now speaks only to our inner ear, reachable through the eye alone. And though the poem returns intermittently to the touchable object and its physical qualities ("The jacket ripped, the spine cracked, / Still it arouses me"), it ends by invoking the intangible. Or rather, it ends with a transubstantiation that mingles the two:

And the passion to make a book—passion of the writer

Smelling glue and ink, sensuous. The writer's dread of making
Another tombstone, my marker orderly in its place in the stacks.

Or to infiltrate and inhabit another soul, as a splinter of spirit
Pressed between pages like a wildflower, odorless, brittle.

Reading this poem, I wondered at first if it would be meaningless to future generations who had read only electronic books. What would they make of those cracked spines, those smells, those pages? Then I realized that, unless history disappears along with books, the meaning of this poem will remain accessible, just as that cartoon about scrolls makes sense to us even if we have never actually seen an ancient scroll. The poem itself could even be part of what helps transmit the past (that is, our present) to the future. In that as-yet-unimaginable time when the visceral pleasures Pinsky describes are all gone, some "splinter" of them will remain in the "odorless, brittle" form of the poet's reported experience.

Such losses happen all the time in literature, and yet we readers manage to transcend them; we manage to continue

getting the joke, despite the disappearance of the circumstances that gave rise to it. I'm thinking now of an actual joke
that occurs in the pages of *Don Quixote*, somewhere near the
beginning of Volume Two. In order to understand the joke,
you have to know that eleven years passed between the publication of the first volume and the appearance of this second
one in 1615, and that during the intervening decade, the
knight and his adventures became famous throughout Spain.
But you don't have to know this before you start reading,
because Volume Two tells you this in its opening pages.
Everyone Don Quixote meets in the second book has heard
of him already, and all these new fans are anxious to see him
do something foolish and chivalric before their very eyes. He
has become the hero of his own novel in a setting that is supposedly outside that novel. The lunatic knight accepts this as
nothing more than his due, but the practical, earthy Sancho
Panza finds the existence of two selves, the "book" self and
the "real" self, confusing and disturbing. He is especially perturbed by one interlocutor, Sansón Carrasco, who insists on
grilling him about the disappearance and then inexplicable
reappearance of the ass he was riding in Part One. Eventually
Sancho just throws up his hands: "'I don't know what answer
to give you,' said Sancho, 'except that the one who wrote the
story must have made a mistake, or else it must be due to
carelessness on the part of the printer.'"

To have a character in a novel talk about that novel's
printing errors when print was relatively new must have been
a startling and witty thing to do. But it seems to me that this
line has remained just as startling and witty over the course
of four centuries. The joke lies, of course, in the character's
impossible perspective, the way he can peer in at his own
story and comment on the shortcomings of the book that
made him. We don't actually have to know how the book

was made to find this funny—we don't have to picture the printer laboriously setting out the rows of metal type and then feeding each page through the press—because no matter *how* it was made, it seems unlikely that this kind of plot flaw could be due to a printer's error. Cervantes is both accepting the blame and winkingly trying to spread it around, so he allows Sancho to seize on any possible alternative to the idea "that the one who wrote the story must have made a mistake." The ploy should feel cheap and obvious, and instead it is vertigo-inducing, as if the lid had been blown off the creative process, and all of its participants—author, character, reader—had shrunk to the same size, or grown to the same size, or at any rate become equals. And the joke works equally well in all the different manifestations of the book. It works whether I am reading *Don Quixote* in my beautiful hardcover edition from 1949, still set in hot type, though on an automated press rather than a hand-driven one; or in my cheaper paperback from 1986, by which time the type would have been set electronically; or in a Project Gutenberg digitalized version, where the very name of the beneficent "publisher" alludes to that technological bombshell of 1450, the invention of movable type, which made printers' errors possible on such a wide scale. I suspect it is a joke that will never die, no matter what happens to the physical form of books.

For an author to forge an intimate connection with you, the book you hold in your hands (or, if hands someday become irrelevant to the process, in your eyes, in your ears, in your mind) need not resemble the actual object he originally put out into the world. And this is true even when he is alluding to that object. Chaucer sends *Troilus and Criseyde* out to us by saying, "Go, litel book, go, litel myn tragedye," but the book in which I read those lines is not little at all: it is a big, fat edition containing all of Geoffrey Chaucer's known works, complete with scholarly apparatus. This is not a problem. It is Chaucer's own voice I hear in this verse, not the editor's or the printer's. Part of the reason we value Chaucer so much, part of the reason we still care about him more than six hundred years after he wrote, lies in the strength and particularity of that voice.

He himself was worried, though, about the process of transmission. He says as much in the stanza that immediately follows the "litel bok" passage:

> And for ther is so gret diversite
> In Englissh and in writyng of oure tonge,
> So prey I God that non myswrite the,
> Ne the mysmetre for defaute of tonge.
> And red wherso thow be, or elles songe,
> That thow be understonde, God I biseche!

There is much less diversity in English now, or at least in its spelling: we would all, these days, "pray . . . that none miswrite thee," or express the hope that the book, "read wheresoever thou be, or else sung, . . . be understood." But despite its orthographic disguise, the protective concern with which Chaucer addresses his little book is still completely understandable, especially if we consider that "books" then were actually manuscripts, each individually copied by a possibly unreliable scribe. The scribes for *Troilus and Criseyde* may even have been worse than average: at any rate, more variants exist for that text than for many of Chaucer's others. According to the editor of my scholarly edition, even the most reliable manuscripts of *Troilus* "contain errors and omissions," and in regard to other revisions or changes, there is "uncertainty whether they are due to Chaucer or a scribe." So the poet was right to be worried. And yet we have received his transmission in its essence, just as generations of us were able to receive Dostoyevsky's *Demons* even with its crucial chapter hacked out by the censors. It's amazing how, against all odds, readers and writers still manage to conjoin.

One more tale about a physical book, and then I am done.

Recently I felt the need to reread Conrad's *Nostromo* in order to verify that I had been correct in describing it as I had, as primarily grand rather than intimate. The copy of that novel sitting on my shelves was a tattered Signet paperback, with an unbelievable seventy-five-cent price printed on its crumpled front cover. Oh, well, I thought, age cannot wither nor custom stale—but I was wrong. Some books are just too old, or too cheaply made, to be worth reading. This one had such narrow margins that the lines of print disappeared into the gutter and I had to crack the spine to read each page. The printing was so shoddy that if I ran a finger across the type—a dry finger, mind you—the black letters slurred together into an illegible smear. I felt sorry for the younger self who had only been able to afford this version of *Nostromo*; I also admired her persistence in getting through it. I tried reading it for one or two chapters, and then I gave up.

I could and did download the novel from Gutenberg, but I knew that even if this temporarily solved my problem, it would not be a permanent fix. *Nostromo* is one of those formative, crucial works of literature I need to have on my actual bookshelves, in my actual library. A bodiless version stored in a digital library will never, for me, be a sufficient replacement. Before I could throw away that crummy paperback, I had to get a solid copy to fill its hole on the shelf. So I once again resorted to online ordering, and with masses of inexpensive used editions to choose from, I bought a Modern Library hardcover, complete with original book jacket and transparent plastic jacket cover, which was rated by its seller as being in "Very Good" condition. It arrived so quickly that I didn't even have time to turn to the Gutenberg version; and since, as should now be obvious, I always prefer a real book if I have it, this is the one I reread.

But I am not going to tell you about that (except to say that I was right the first time: the novel *is* grand rather than intimate). The point of my tale is what happened when I finished reading. I held the pleasant weight of the closed book for a moment in my hands, as if to bid its story a silent goodbye, and then I turned it over. On the back cover of that 1951 edition of *Nostromo*—older than I am by a year, and therefore deriving from some romantic, insufficiently imaginable past era—was an ad announcing that "The best of the world's best books are now available in the inexpensive, compact, definitive editions of the Modern Library." The phrase "Modern Library" was in a large, turquoise, semicursive typeface that must have seemed the height of modernity in 1951; and the same blue color appeared in the jacket's upper-left corner, in the form of a small pointing hand, the kind of printer's dingbat you might associate with nineteenth-century posters for magic shows or healing nostrums. Its index finger was aimed at the words: SEE INSIDE OF JACKET FOR COMPLETE LIST OF TITLES.

I am nothing if not obedient, so I removed the jacket from the book and carefully unwrapped the Plasti-Kleen Quik-Fold cover that was concealing its inner surface. A fragile, thin, parchment-colored sheet containing seven finely printed columns was revealed. The headline above this hidden treasure said, "Which of these 352 outstanding books do you want to read?" and the list itself ran from "Adams, Henry, *The Education of Henry Adams*" at the top of the first column to "Zweig, Stefan, *Amok*" at the bottom of the seventh. It was a wonderful list. It included "Marx, Karl, *Capital and*

Other Writings" (this in 1951, at the height of the red-baiting McCarthy era) and "Veblen, Thorstein, *The Theory of the Leisure Class*." Plato, Aristotle, Suetonius, and Thucydides were all here; so were Machiavelli, Kant, and Nietzsche. There were four novels by Henry James, as well as four by Conrad, four by Faulkner, three by Dickens, and three by D. H. Lawrence. The first six translated volumes of Marcel Proust appeared here, as well as numerous other translations from the French (Balzac, Montaigne, Voltaire, Zola), Russian (Dostoyevsky, Gogol, Tolstoy, Turgenev), Italian (Boccaccio, Dante), German (Freud, Goethe), Spanish (Cervantes), Norwegian (Knut Hamsun), and even Chinese (Confucius). There were plays as well: not just the complete Shakespeare, but also Molière, Ibsen, Eugene O'Neill, Oscar Wilde, and a number of dramatic anthologies. And there was poetry, ranging from Emily Dickinson and Robert Frost through Homer and Keats to Virgil, Wordsworth, and Yeats. Perhaps most surprisingly, these broad-minded editors had even included a few works from despised genres in their "outstanding" list: an anthology called *Three Famous Murder Novels*, for instance, and another called *Great Tales of Terror and the Supernatural*.

Of course, there were oddities. There always are, in such cases, not just because of personal tastes, but also because each period has its own preferences which mask the oddities for a time, making them seem logical and even predictable. In 1951, it made sense to include John Marquand, S. J. Perelman, and Ogden Nash on a list that would no doubt exclude them today. Erskine Caldwell, Daphne du Maurier, and Dorothy Parker were all represented—indeed, overrepresented, with two or three titles each—and though I consider myself a partisan of both Somerset Maugham and John Steinbeck, I would have to say there was a bit too much of them as well. Hemingway was there, but Fitzgerald was missing; Max

Beerbohm made an appearance, whereas Ford Madox Ford did not. And strange, now-obscure historians and biographers (Francis Hackett, Emil Ludwig, Dmitri Merejkowski, Hendrik van Loon) were sprinkled here and there like so many nearly effaced tombstones.

But that is not only normal for a list of this kind; it is inevitable, if the list-makers are doing their job properly. It does no good simply to recommend the carefully plucked, time-approved choices of the past. Reading, if it is to stay alive, must be of its time as well as out of it. New literature that is worth preserving is coming into being every day, and older works that were once ignored are constantly making their way back into print, but from our own fixed position in history, we can't be expected to know for sure which are the ones that will endure.

Nothing worth saying, in such a situation, can be guaranteed to remain permanently true. No list, no opinion, however valid in its own time, will last forever. But that does not mean the attempt is not worth the paper it is written on (or whatever measure of value will arise when paper is no longer with us). To me, a list like the valiant, generous Modern Library one is intensely moving, even in its misjudgments. The point is to make a stab at it—at sharing the individual and collective wisdom, at assessing what matters and what does not—and then to abide with the consequences. In the never-ending conversation about what might count as good literature, there are many worse things than being wrong.

A HUNDRED BOOKS

TO READ FOR PLEASURE

This is not supposed to be a list of the hundred best books. Some of the very best books in the world (*Paradise Lost, Remembrance of Things Past, The Oresteia, Don Quixote,* to name just a few of the obvious ones) do not appear here at all. I don't want us to get bogged down aiming for coverage. This is not a literary canon, and there will be no final exam—for any of us. No one is going to ask us on our deathbeds how many great books we've read, and at that point even *we* won't care. Reading is not about progressing toward a finish line, any more than life is.

The idea is simply to offer you a list of books that have all brought me great pleasure in the course of my life. Because we are not the same person, your tastes will differ from mine, and these books will not all give you the same delight they gave me. I cannot predict which ones will fail you—you will just have to give them a try, and if you find yourself getting bored, quit that book and go on to the next. There is nothing shameful about giving up on a book in the middle: that is the exercise of taste.

And remember, there are always more where these came from. I limited myself to one title per author, which means that for every book named here, there could be three or eight or thirty by the same writer that you might enjoy just as much. Once you find an author whose work appeals to you, you can mine that lode until it's exhausted. Or, if you prefer, you can save up all her remaining works for a rainy day. How you go about it is entirely up to you.

Choosing which book should represent each author was a difficult and unsettling process. I felt, for instance, that I practically had to list *The Way We Live Now* for Trollope, since it is clearly his finest novel—but does this mean you will fail to read *Phineas Finn*, or *He Knew He Was Right*, or any of the other terrific books he left us? Why did I pick Dostoyevsky's *Crime and Punishment* over *The Idiot* or *Demons* or *The Brothers Karamazov*, all of which I love just as much? Was I depriving you of the true D. H. Lawrence by giving you his best novel, *Sons and Lovers*, rather than his best nonfiction book, *Studies in Classic American Literature*? Did the brilliant intensity of Melville's shorter fiction make up for the fact that it was usurping the place of his masterpiece, *Moby-Dick*? And how could *any* single work stand in for all the marvelously satisfying novels written by my dear Henry James?

Then there are the missing. William Empson and Randall Jarrell were here in an earlier version of this list. So was John le Carré. So was Stefan Zweig. I still regret their absence. I still wonder if you might have liked *Milton's God* or *The Third Book of Criticism* or *A Perfect Spy* or *The Post-Office Girl* better than whatever finally went into those slots. And then there are my contemporaries and near-contemporaries, so many of whom are absent. It would have given me pleasure to recommend Michael Chabon's *The Yiddish Policemen's Union*, Kay Ryan's *The Best of It*, Peter Carey's *My Life as a Fake*, Julian Barnes's *Arthur & George*, and Zadie Smith's *NW*, among others; but I felt you would already know about those authors, whereas older books by now-dead writers were more in need of my championing. Having set my arbitrary limit of a hundred books (which is not *so* arbitrary, if you are a ten-digited human), I felt obliged to adhere to it. So excruciating excisions and hesitant substitutions continued to take place during the entire time I was writing this book. If I am through with them now, it is only because my time is up. Composing a list like this is one of those tasks that can be stopped but never finished, and now it is up to you to carry on, which is why I have left some white space at the end.

Ackerley, J. R., *My Father and Myself*
Ambler, Eric, *A Coffin for Dimitrios*
Austen, Jane, *Persuasion*
Baldwin, James, *Notes of a Native Son*
Balzac, Honoré, *Cousin Bette*
Bellow, Saul, *Ravelstein*
Bennett, Arnold, *The Old Wives' Tale*
Bishop, Elizabeth, *The Complete Poems*
Bolaño, Roberto, *Distant Star*
Bowen, Elizabeth, *The Heat of the Day*
Carroll, Lewis, *Alice's Adventures in Wonderland*
Cather, Willa, *The Professor's House*
Chekhov, Anton, *The Lady with the Dog and Other Stories*
Coetzee, J. M., *Disgrace*
Collins, Wilkie, *The Woman in White*
Conrad, Joseph, *Under Western Eyes*
de Waal, Edmund, *The Hare with Amber Eyes*
Der Nister, *The Family Mashber*
Dickens, Charles, *David Copperfield*
Dickinson, Emily, *Final Harvest*
Dostoyevsky, Fyodor, *Crime and Punishment*
Dyer, Geoff, *Out of Sheer Rage*

Eisenberg, Deborah, *Twilight of the Superheroes*
Elkin, Stanley, *Van Gogh's Room at Arles*
Ellison, Ralph, *Invisible Man*
Farrell, J. G., *The Siege of Krishnapur*
Faulkner, William, *Absalom, Absalom!*
Fitzgerald, Penelope, *The Beginning of Spring*
Flaubert, Gustave, *Sentimental Education*
Fontane, Theodor, *Effi Briest*
Ford, Ford Madox, *Parade's End*
Ford, Richard, *The Bascombe Novels*
Forster, E. M., *A Passage to India*
Gissing, George, *New Grub Street*
Glück, Louise, *A Village Life*
Gogol, Nikolai, *Collected Tales*
Goncharov, Ivan, *Oblomov*
Greene, Graham, *The Quiet American*
Grossman, Vasily, *Life and Fate*
Gunn, Thom, *Collected Poems*
Handke, Peter, *A Sorrow Beyond Dreams*
Hardwick, Elizabeth, *The Simple Truth*
Hardy, Thomas, *Jude the Obscure*
Hazzard, Shirley, *The Transit of Venus*
Heaney, Seamus, *The Haw Lantern*
Herzen, Alexander, *My Past and Thoughts*
Highsmith, Patricia, *The Complete Ripley Novels*
Hopkins, Gerard Manley, *Poems*
Howells, William Dean, *A Hazard of New Fortunes*
James, Henry, *The Golden Bowl*
Lahiri, Jhumpa, *Unaccustomed Earth*
Lampedusa, Giuseppe di, *The Leopard*
Lawrence, D. H., *Sons and Lovers*
Li, Yiyun, *Gold Boy, Emerald Girl*
London, Jack, *Martin Eden*

Lowell, Robert, *Life Studies*
Macdonald, Ross, *The Blue Hammer*
Mailer, Norman, *The Armies of the Night*
Malcolm, Janet, *In the Freud Archives*
Malouf, David, *The Great World*
Mankell, Henning, *Sidetracked*
Mann, Thomas, *Buddenbrooks*
Mantel, Hilary, *Beyond Black*
Marías, Javier, *A Heart So White*
Maxwell, William, *So Long, See You Tomorrow*
McEwan, Ian, *The Innocent*
Melville, Herman, *Great Short Works*
Michaels, Leonard, *Collected Stories*
Mistry, Rohinton, *A Fine Balance*
Munro, Alice, *Friend of My Youth*
Murakami, Haruki, *Hard-boiled Wonderland and the End of the World*
Norris, Frank, *The Pit*
O'Connor, Flannery, *Wise Blood*
Ondaatje, Michael, *Running in the Family*
Orwell, George, *The Road to Wigan Pier*
Pinsky, Robert, *Selected Poems*
Platonov, Andrey, *Soul and Other Stories*
Price, Richard, *Clockers*
Roth, Joseph, *The Radetzky March*
Roth, Philip, *I Married a Communist*
Rushdie, Salman, *The Moor's Last Sigh*
Queirós, Eça de, *The Maias*
Sebald, W. G., *The Rings of Saturn*
Serge, Victor, *The Case of Comrade Tulayev*
Stafford, Jean, *The Mountain Lion*
Stendhal, *The Charterhouse of Parma*
Svevo, Italo, *Zeno's Conscience*

Theroux, Paul, *The Family Arsenal*
Tóibín, Colm, *The Master*
Tolstoy, Leo, *War and Peace*
Trevor, William, *The Children of Dynmouth*
Trollope, Anthony, *The Way We Live Now*
Turgenev, Ivan, *Virgin Soil*
Twain, Mark, *Huckleberry Finn*
Verne, Jules, *The Mysterious Island*
West, Rebecca, *The Fountain Overflows*
Wharton, Edith, *The House of Mirth*
Wolff, Tobias, *In Pharaoh's Army*
Wright, Richard, *Native Son*
Zola, Émile, *The Ladies' Paradise*

ACKNOWLEDGMENTS

This book would not have been possible without the intelligent and useful advice of Arthur Lubow, Katharine Michaels, Thomas Wong, Tim Clark, Anne Wagner, and, above all, Ileene Smith.

INDEX